How To Romanticise Your Life

The Ultimate Guide to Living Your Desired Reality

Honor Lewis

Disclaimer

The information in this book is not in any way a substitution for receiving conventional medical or professional treatment or consulting a physician. All the practices in this book are to be used as an addition to existing treatments to assist the healing process and should be fully explored only in conjunction with suitable training. Neither the author or publication assumes any liability at all for any damages caused through the application or misapplication of procedures and statements in this book.

Dedication

To the lady who gave me the book on that spring day. I would not have any of this knowledge or be on this journey if it wasn't for you.

I also want to thank Matthew, being there for me throughout the process of writing this book. Encouraging me, supporting me, and sharing my excitement. I wouldn't have got this far without you.

Contents

Doing the "Hard Work"

Live Your Best Life Now

How to Romanticise Your Career

My Story, My Mission.

Introduction

Have you ever watched a romantic comedy or any happy movie and thought to yourself, "I wish this were my life," or "If only real life were like this"? I know I have. Personally, I've always been told that such scenarios were 'unattainable' or 'simply not real life.' Hearing those words, I, like many others, just moved on. Throughout life, I've noticed that people often receive unwarranted advice about how things are supposed to be. In most cases, the recipients of this advice would listen and accept these words, especially after experiencing a setback.

While growing up, we often draw significant influence from our parents or guardians. I recall a class activity in primary school when I was six, where I was asked, "What do you want to do when you grow up?" I confidently responded that I wanted to be a shopkeeper like my Mummy. However, as I reached the age of ten, my aspirations shifted towards becoming an architect, inspired by a part of my Dad's profession. At that young age, those were the occupations I knew most about. Though I was aware of other jobs, I hadn't witnessed them firsthand like I had with my parents' occupations, so they didn't really register as options in my mind.

Similarly, when we are young, the words of those we look up to hold immense weight. We trust that what they tell us is the absolute truth, and our opinions and thoughts are shaped accordingly. Reflecting on those moments, I realise how impressionable children are and how heavily they rely on being taught about the ways of the world. As we grow older, the question arises: "What is the right thing to teach our children?" if we choose to have any, of course. However, the process doesn't stop there. We progress to high school, forming our own ideologies, yet even then, they are influenced by our peers and experiences. This can be highly beneficial, as we learn about the world through diverse perspectives and encounter ideologies we would never have discovered on our own. However, like everything, there are downsides.

Have you ever considered that what you are being told may potentially limit you?

For some individuals, when they express their aspirations of becoming a famous actor or actress, they may encounter discouragement from others, often from someone they trust or consider an authority figure. These individuals may hear statements like, "It's extremely difficult to find success; it requires a lot of luck," or "You'll probably end up as a drama teacher because finding work in the industry is tough." While these comments may stem from good intentions, they reflect the personal experiences and learned beliefs of the person offering them. Unfortunately, such influences can prematurely extinguish a person's dream.

Following our dreams, living a fulfilling life, and pursuing our desires can be challenging when others dictate how life should be lived. It's important to recognise that these individuals aren't necessarily to blame. We all come from different backgrounds and experiences that shape our perspectives. I have personally noticed common mindsets that include notions such as "only lucky people achieve success," "you must work excessively hard," or "only the very best can make it." These are just a few examples, but the list goes on.

Now, I want to go into the purpose behind writing this book. I have endured difficult periods in my life that I can confidently say were the toughest times I've faced, filled with regrets and hardships. However, through those experiences, I have learned valuable lessons about myself, embarked on a journey of healing from the past, and discovered new insights that I couldn't keep to myself. I wanted to share a fresh perspective, one that you can choose to embrace or disregard— it's entirely up to you.

The only difference is that I am still in the process of fully establishing myself, but I am on the right path and have achieved significant milestones. I didn't want to wait solely because I felt the need to prove myself materially, so I decided to write this book now. It is dedicated to you, the reader, whoever you may be.

The purpose of this book is to convey to the world that no matter how challenging life may become and regardless of the experiences you encounter, there are ways to infuse a touch of magic into it, to find enjoyment, and to realise that no matter what happens, there are small actions you can take to make life feel a little bit better.

My Story

To begin, I will discuss the period in my life when things became challenging. Let me clarify that I had a good childhood, and my parents made every effort to support my family. I am immensely grateful to them. However, like many individuals, I faced some difficult moments. Before I continue, I want to provide a trigger warning, as I will briefly touch upon sensitive topics.

Before I go into my personal story, I want to emphasise the purpose of sharing it with you. I have discovered that it often took going through multiple unpleasant experiences during my early life to teach me valuable lessons and foster personal growth. By reflecting on these lessons and gaining new insights about myself, I have been shaped into the person I am today. Recognising the past is essential in understanding how far we have come, and through this section, I aim to demonstrate that, regardless of what you have endured, your upbringing, or even your current circumstances, there is always an opportunity to create something meaningful and live life on your own terms. I firmly believe that we all deserve that chance. Now, let me recount my experiences.

At a very young age, starting from the age of six to be precise, I was sexually harassed from kids in my class. During that time, I was completely unaware of the nature of the situation, and I didn't attach much significance to it. However, as I reflect on those experiences, I now understand the gravity of what occurred and recognise that it was a harmful and inappropriate situation. Nevertheless, my primary concern shifted towards the circumstances that might have influenced the child involved to engage in such behaviour at such a young age. I have since moved beyond those events and have found it in my heart to forgive them. However, there was a stage in my life when I deeply contemplated these experiences, and I will talk more about that later in this chapter.

This wasn't the only thing that happened. Later, when I was about eight, I was subjected to bullying by many of my classmates. They would repeatedly tell me that I smelled and that I was overweight, and it did make me feel sad. Fortunately, I had a close group of friends who stood by me, and we supported each other through it. In all honesty, I don't dwell on those memories much. However, upon reflection, I believe that a significant portion of my classmates joined in the bullying because it became a trend, and they followed suit. But at the time, it was an unsettling experience. I have forgiven everyone involved. I'm grateful that the bullying stopped the following year. Things seemed to settle down for me (to the best of my memory) until I reached around the age of 14.

Obviously, as a teenage girl, I was under the impression that I was becoming an adult and believed I had all the answers, when in reality, I was still discovering the ways of the world. Relationships started to intrigue me as I observed my friends entering into relationships. At the time, I was rather shy and spent a significant amount of time gaming and being active online. It was during this period that I encountered an individual through a game, who claimed to be my age, and we developed a friendship that evolved into an "online relationship." Interestingly, when I reflect on it now, I don't consider it a genuine relationship, so I don't give it much thought. Returning to the story, everything seemed fine initially, but there were warning signs that I failed to recognise at the time. For instance, whenever I asked him for a photo taken with a camera, he would provide excuses like "my camera is broken," "it shows an error," or he would swiftly change the subject. It was a major "red flag" and deep down, I had a gut feeling that he was likely not genuine. However, I found it challenging to distance myself, possibly due to manipulation or other factors I can't recall precisely. I experienced a sense of being "loved" for the first time, and I feel that was the reason it was hard to cut ties. I am very relieved that I eventually summoned the strength and courage to break free from that situation. Looking back now, I feel a sense of pride in myself. I am grateful for this experience as it has provided me with valuable lessons and growth. Since then, I have completely avoided situations of being catfished and maybe even groomed.

The final significant "tragedy" in my life was the separation of my parents, which also had a profound impact on my siblings. This event affected me deeply because I had always suppressed my emotions, rarely allowing myself to cry or acknowledge when I wasn't okay. However, when my parents split, everything came crashing down. Years of bottled-up emotions took their toll on me in an overwhelming way.

Suddenly, I felt burdened by all my problems, and I spiralled into a deep depression. I felt a sense of hopelessness and became extremely self-critical. I fixated on the negative aspects of my life and convinced myself that it would always be that way. I disregarded the positive experiences and failed to see their significance. I ended up placing blame on my Dad, believing that if my parents hadn't separated, everything would have been fine. It's difficult for me to admit that this mindset caused a great deal of problems and has left me with many regrets. Depression can distort one's perception and lead to irrational thoughts and behaviours.

The silver lining during that challenging period was my recognition of my depression and taking the initiative to seek counselling. Although it was a lengthy process, I eventually secured the support I needed. Opening up and discussing my past experiences for the first time proved to be difficult, and I must admit that things got worse before they got better. There was a period when I engaged in self-harming behaviours and experienced thoughts of suicide. However, as time went on, I started to experience improvement. While I wasn't yet feeling completely restored, I began to see a glimmer of hope for the future.

When I turned 16, towards the end of 2016, my first round of counselling came to an end. However, one evening while I was looking at my childhood photos, something strange occurred.

Initially, it was a pleasant experience gazing at the images, but gradually, a sense of unease overwhelmed me. It was as if a panic attack was building up inside me, yet I knew it wasn't exactly that. I vividly remember rushing outside in search of my Mum, who was out walking the dogs. She had to constantly keep me distracted to help me cope with these overwhelmingly anxious feelings. Looking back, I believe I had an emotional breakdown during that moment. The following day, when I went to school, I experienced a new sensation—an emotion I had never felt before, but I recognised it as anxiety.

It was a distressing period, and I constantly lived in fear. After enduring this for a month, I decided to seek counselling once again. Thankfully, my family and friends provided unwavering support and assistance as I battled daily anxiety attacks. I found myself avoiding various activities due to overwhelming fear and discomfort. The persistence of my anxiety issues weighed heavily on me, and it even began to manifest physical symptoms, affecting my stomach and overall well-being. Coping with these challenges became increasingly difficult. Throughout this journey, I worked with a total of four counsellors and underwent cognitive behavioural therapy (CBT) to address my anxiety.

These approaches certainly aided my progress, but I wouldn't attribute them as the sole factors that "fixed me." By using the term "fixed me" in quotation marks, I have occasional bouts of anxiety still currently arise in my life, but I now possess full control over my body. While I pursued various methods, such as medication and therapy, to help my healing process, they served as helpful tools rather than definitive cures.

There is a particular memory I cherish, which also happens to be the most movie-like experience of my life. Whenever I recount this story, my listeners are often amazed, and some even question if it is real, due to its surreal nature. Allow me to share what unfolded on that remarkable occasion...

One Miracle that Started it all.

I remember completing my first year of A-Levels, and one warm, beautiful spring day, I had a photography class. It was during a time when I experienced daily anxiety. As I walked to the bus stop, the warm sun touched my skin, and I couldn't help but appreciate the blooming flowers, the trees adorned with pink blossoms, and the delightful sound of birds chirping. I felt fortunate to live in the countryside, surrounded by such natural beauty. These were moments I truly cherished, especially before having to face the uneasiness that awaited me in my class.

I sat at the bus stop for a moment, and a lady sat down next to me, striking up a conversation. She asked me the usual questions like whether I was in college and what course I was studying. I shared with her that I had started my final photography project, focusing on mysteries. As I explained that I was in the research stage of this project, she mentioned, "I have a good book about secrets and mysteries." Surprisingly, she lived near me and suggested that I visit her house after finishing college to receive the book. The bus arrived shortly after, and I carried on with my day, not thinking much of her offer at the time.

The day at college finally came to an end, and I must admit that I had completely forgotten about her offer. Boarding the bus, to my surprise, I spotted her sitting by the window, waving at me, and signalling for me to join her. I took a seat beside her, and we shared a laugh about the coincidence of crossing paths again. During the 10-minute bus ride, we engaged in casual conversation. Upon reaching our stop, we walked to her house, and she quickly retrieved the book for me. When I asked her when she would like it back, she insisted I keep it. Grateful, I thanked her and made my way back home.

I reached my doorstep, turned the key, entered my house, and settled down. I took out the book, instantly captivated by its eye-catching orange cover. The title, "The Power" by Rhonda Byrne, intrigued me, especially since it was a sequel to her book named "The Secret." Initially, I wondered how this book about the power could relate to mysteries or aid me with my photography project. Curiously, I delved into the blurb and found myself deeply fascinated by its content. The book introduced the concept of The Law of Attraction and how it can help individuals manifest their dream lives. Prior to this, I had never encountered the Law of Attraction or its ideology. The closest concept I knew was probably "treat others how you want to be treated," which I learned during my primary school days.

I eagerly opened the book and immersed myself in its pages, studying its contents. Chapter after chapter, I went deeper into its teachings, spending a good hour, or so engrossed in its wisdom. It was during this time that a metaphorical lightbulb switched on in my mind. I must admit, the book had a profound impact on my life, as if it had unlocked a dormant understanding within me.

In retrospect, I can see it as the beacon of hope I had always yearned for. As a discontented teenager navigating through college, I felt lost and directionless, desperately seeking guidance. The book presented various techniques, including utilising the law of attraction, raising my vibration, and cultivating gratitude. Intrigued, I decided to apply these principles in my life, and to my surprise, they worked remarkably well. Seven years have passed, and I continue to incorporate these practices.

Initially, my primary focus was to infuse positivity into my life and overcome my anxiety. At the time, it seemed like an insurmountable task, but I maintained an open mind. The book offered numerous insights and tips, which initially posed a challenge in assimilating all the information and determining the best course of action.

The core principle I derived from the book was the importance of focusing on the positive aspects of life. The following day, I put this idea into practice by consciously directing my attention towards the good things and cultivating positive thoughts. The sunny weather provided the perfect backdrop for my experiment, and I revelled in the joy it brought me. I took in the beauty of the flowers, the vibrant green grass, the warmth in the air, the ambient sounds, and the gentle caress of the breeze against my skin. It had been a while since I had felt such serenity.

Initially, it was a bit challenging, as if I were reprogramming my mind to actively seek out the sources of happiness rather than succumbing to my anxieties. I carried this approach into my class as well, focusing on the things that brought me joy. As a result, I had an exceptionally good day— a rarity in recent times. The key factor that contributed to this positive shift was staying grounded in the present moment, disregarding negative thoughts, and reclaiming control over my own state of being. By immersing myself in the present and fully appreciating the goodness that surrounded me, which I had previously overlooked, I experienced a sense of liberation. It felt as if I had discovered a hidden facet of life that had been right in front of me all along.

It is safe to say that receiving that book has had a profound impact on my life, fundamentally transforming the way I live for the better. Interestingly, while I didn't utilise it directly for my photography project, it served as a catalyst for shaping my entire existence. The book taught me invaluable lessons, prompting me to embark on a personal journey to create the life I truly desired.

As time passed, I journeyed deeper into my quest for knowledge. The book served as a starting point, and from there, I conducted my own research and experimented with various techniques. I embarked on a spiritual journey, initially keeping it private, where I discovered concepts such as the 3D and 5D ways of living. This exploration allowed me to become more attuned to my intuition and experience several spiritual awakenings.

Now, six years later, I can confidently say that I have encountered happiness, triumphed over challenges, and embraced an entirely new perspective on life—one influenced by positivity, unconditional love, and an appreciation for the small, simple, yet remarkable aspects of existence. I have reached a state of genuine contentment, and my happiness is rooted in the choices I make and the way I perceive the world around me.

I have been fortunate enough to encounter remarkable opportunities that I attribute to the hardships I have endured in the past. In sharing a brief summary of my experiences, my intention is to convey my firm belief that regardless of one's past or current circumstances, it is possible to overcome adversity and embrace the role of creator in shaping one's own life. Each and every person possesses the inherent power to pursue their heart's truest desires.

At times, our minds can be influenced by the weight of our past, prompting us to make decisions based on logic and safety rather than following our passions. However, I firmly believe that every hardship we encounter serves as a valuable lesson and contributes to the unique individuals we have become today. These experiences shape us and grant us the wisdom and resilience necessary to navigate the journey of life.

No matter what challenges we face, we have the capacity to rise above them, transform our circumstances, and lead a life that aligns with our deepest aspirations. It is through embracing these lessons and experiences that we can unlock our true potential and lead a fulfilling and purposeful existence.

The struggles I have personally endured have ultimately led me to write this book and explore a new perspective on life that brings joy. My primary goal is to share what has worked for me in the hopes that it can positively impact the lives of others. Even if this book only helps one person, even in the slightest way, it will bring me immense joy. However, I also recognise that if it doesn't resonate with everyone, that's perfectly alright because I have still had the opportunity to share my thoughts and insights with you.

Having provided you with a brief glimpse into my personal history, let us now return to the present moment. What is my mission for writing this book? What knowledge can you expect to gain from reading it? The upcoming chapter will go into these aspects and provide you with a deeper understanding of the purpose behind this book.

My mission

To put it simply, I have always contemplated how the world would be transformed if individuals were consistently happy, pursuing their dreams, and engaging in activities they truly loved. I understand that achieving such a state might seem nearly impossible. However, it has been a persistent thought in my mind, and I have often wondered how I could contribute to making it a reality.

I noticed how, as a child, people would often complain about their lives, and I would wonder why adults couldn't simply do something to improve their situations. However, as I've grown up and gained firsthand experience, I now understand that it's not as simple as it seemed. If someone were to ask you right now how to make your life better, most people wouldn't have a clear answer. It can be challenging to figure out how to improve your life while you're still navigating its difficulties. With this book, I aim to provide you with a step-by-step process to take a step back, reflect, and discover simple yet effective ways to either find enjoyment in your current life or make it even better. The approach I take involves asking thought-provoking questions to help you identify what you truly want and then motivating you to make small changes in your life. It's important to keep these changes manageable, as attempting to drastically transform your life can lead to overwhelm or a sense of it being too much work, discouraging you from taking action.

Finally, I want to introduce you to some elements that may be new to you, such as the law of attraction, which goes hand in hand with romanticising your life. These concepts can help you achieve and attain things you have always desired but perhaps thought were out of reach.

The last section of this book is divided into three categories: career, relationships, and home life. Each section focuses individually on how you can infuse romanticism and joy into these areas of your life. By the end of this book, you will hopefully feel inspired and have a clear vision of the steps you can take to experience pure enjoyment in your life.

There is a sparkle in life that everyone deserves to experience. We are here on this earth, in this current lifetime, with the opportunity to make the most out of it. There is so much beauty to witness and experience, and it is within your reach.

Life presents us with tough moments, but we can use them as opportunities for expansion, growth, and becoming the best versions of ourselves. It is never too late to start cultivating happiness and fulfilment in your life, and this book can serve as a starting point for you.

Romanticising Your Life

What does it mean to romanticise your life?

Let's start with a brief history lesson. During the 18th Century in Europe, an artistic movement called Romanticism emerged. It encompassed various forms of expression, including art, literature, music, and intellectual pursuits.

"Romanticism emphasized the individual, the subjective, the irrational, the imaginative, the personal, the spontaneous, the emotional, the visionary, and the transcendental." (Romanticism | Definition, Characteristics, Artists, History, Art, Poetry, Literature, & Music, 2022)

The romantics of that era held a deep appreciation for nature, placing great importance on their emotions and senses. They prioritised their passions and embraced their role as creators, diverging from the conventional paths that were typically followed during that time.

When exploring the idea of how to romanticise one's life in the present day, it closely aligns with this concept. Some refer to it as "living life as the main character," where you intentionally embrace the life you desire and find beauty even in the ordinary moments. The specifics of romanticising life vary for each individual. To demonstrate, let me share my own example. For me, a romanticised life involves appreciating the world's beauty and the inherent value of life itself. It entails understanding myself on a spiritual and emotional level and allowing those aspects to shape the path I choose. Additionally, being creative and pursuing my interests are crucial components. By incorporating these elements, I can confidently say that I am living my best life. However, the definition of a romanticised life may differ significantly for someone else.

When delving into the realm of romanticism, it's essential to acknowledge that not everything can or should be romanticised. It's easy to put on "rose-tinted glasses" and overlook negative situations. A prime example of this is dealing with toxic individuals in your life. There may be someone with ill intentions who mistreats you, failing to provide the respect and care you deserve. If taken to an extreme, romanticism may blind you to this reality, causing you to ignore or overlook the person's harmful behaviour and only focus on their positive traits. This can become problematic. In such situations, a more balanced approach to romanticism would involve standing up for yourself, similar to how a main character in a story would and cutting out toxic individuals from your life.

The same caution applies when it comes to mental health. Some individuals might use romanticism as a means of escaping their mental health challenges, avoiding the need to confront and address them. While finding beauty and joy in life is important, it's equally vital to face one's mental health struggles head-on and seek appropriate support and solutions. Romanticism should not be used as a means of evading or neglecting one's mental well-being.

This is something that I highly discourage. We don't want to be ignorant of what is going on in life, especially the negative aspects. In fact, it is important to be aware. Instead, the concept of romanticising your life should be used to find joy in the simple things, bring excitement to your life, and shape it according to your desires. The idea of romanticising your life, as presented in this book, is about taking action, and making changes, whether big or small, to enhance your enjoyment of life.

Overall, romanticism is a subjective concept that varies from person to person. In this book, I aim to demonstrate how to infuse simple, mundane activities and tasks with a sense of romanticism, so that your life doesn't feel monotonous and the ordinary becomes more fulfilling, offering small pleasures to look forward to.

If you're unsure of how you'd like to embrace a romantic approach to life, let's try the following activity.

Grab some paper and a pen, and put on a film that you enjoy, preferably one with romantic elements. Pay attention to how the characters enjoy their daily tasks and navigate through life. A personal favourite of mine for this activity is "Snow White and the Seven Dwarfs," as it showcases the protagonist finding ways to stay optimistic and derive enjoyment from what might be considered mundane tasks.

As you watch your chosen film, jot down elements that you find "beautiful" and would like to incorporate into your own life. Don't worry about realism or if it's possible to do at this stage; simply keep an open mind and list everything that appeals to you. Additionally, feel free to write down any other aspirations or ideas that come to mind, even if they are not directly related to the film you're watching.

Here are a few examples:

- *Singing while cleaning.*
- *Dancing around to music.*
- *Standing in the rain feeling it fall on you.*
- *Sitting in the countryside listening to birdsong.*

- *Laying down counting clouds.*
- *Standing by the window observing the world by drinking tea.*
- *Daydream about all of your desires.*
- *Cooking your favourite food.*
- *Buy yourself flowers.*
- *Walk in nature.*
- *Have a date with yourself.*
- *Watch the sunrise.*
- *Reading a good book in a café.*

The examples I've provided may seem "small" and easily achievable, and upon reflection, you might have noticed that they are. However, in today's society, these activities are often viewed as time-wasting, and we often become so caught up in the fast-paced nature of life that we fail to slow down and appreciate the simple joys it offers. Some may even dismiss these ideas as "silly" or "childish," as they deviate from societal norms. As we grow older, there is a significant societal pressure to "grow up," be mature, and conform to the expectations of adulthood. While this pressure can be beneficial in some respects, it often leads us to abandon the small pleasures we once enjoyed in our youth.

In psychology, there is a concept known as the inner child, which represents the younger aspects of ourselves and often reflects our childlike qualities. This concept can delve into deep psychological territory and is linked to how individuals navigate various situations. In cases where childhood trauma has occurred, it may negatively impact a person's ability to cope with certain situations, and seeking professional help can be beneficial in such instances. However, in the context of this book, we are focusing on the positive aspects and embracing life through our inner child.

During our younger years, if we were fortunate, the world was filled with wonder and excitement. We viewed everything through a different lens compared to our current perspective. If we had a joyful and playful childhood, part of romanticising our lives involves reconnecting with that sense of wonder and joy.

Now, let's revisit your list and reflect on the innocent things you once enjoyed during your childhood. Remember how you may have talked to animals, embarked on explorations, and lived a life filled with wonder. Perhaps there were aspirations you had but were unable to fulfil at that time. Include these on your list. Why not consider incorporating some of those elements into your life now? This isn't about regressing into childhood and abandoning adult responsibilities, but rather about integrating simple and manageable pleasures into your daily life to make it more enjoyable.

Another approach is to think about characters in books or films who possess qualities that you would describe as childlike. They may view life with wonder, experience genuine happiness, or simply remain authentic and true to themselves. I believe that to romanticise your life, it means being true to yourself and living life on your own terms, regardless of what others may say, while still exercising reason and responsibility, of course.

At this point, you likely have a list of things you wish to incorporate into your life. In the following chapters of this book, I will guide you on how to take action and turn these desires into reality. For now, why not tuck that sheet of paper into the book, perhaps as a bookmark, as a reminder of your aspirations? Now that we have an understanding of what it means to romanticise your life, let's begin taking the steps towards embracing this new way of living. You are about to gain insights on how this book will provide guidance for achieving all that you desire and living your life to the fullest. So, let's dive into the fundamentals of romanticising your life.

Getting Started with Romanticising Your Life

Getting to know yourself

When asked the question of "Who are you?", your first instinct is to mention your name, perhaps your age, where you're from, and maybe your occupation. But do these things truly define you? What truly matters about you are your passions, core values, and what excites you. Often, we can get caught up in the busyness of life and the influence of others, forgetting to take time for ourselves, introspect, and truly discover who we are. If you haven't done that before, this chapter provides the perfect opportunity to embark on that journey.

It's essential to set aside dedicated time for yourself, free from external influences, to dive deeper and uncover what brings you joy. By doing so, you'll be able to set meaningful goals aligned with your authentic self and create the life you genuinely desire. This exploration requires finding out what you truly want, not merely what you feel obligated to do or what others expect from you. To assist you in this process, I've prepared some thought-provoking questions for self-reflection. Take your time in answering them, as you want to dig deep within. Once you've formulated your answers, revisit them, considering what your heart truly desires. Feel free to choose the questions that resonate most with you, and answer as many as you wish.

1. *What do you love about your life?*
2. *When are you at your happiest?*
3. *What do you enjoy doing daily?*
4. *What steps are you taking to reach your goals?*
5. *Do you love yourself? If so, what do you love?*
6. *How can you bring more love to yourself daily?*
7. *Describe your perfect day?*
8. *If you could relive any moment, what would it be?*
9. *How do you want to feel and what can you do to feel this?*
10. *What does happiness mean to you?*
11. *What does success mean to you?*
12. *What are you excited for?*

13. *What does self-care mean to you? What does it look like?*
14. *Have you unintentionally set any limits for yourself?*
15. *What does it mean for you to achieve your desires?*

By answering these questions, you are returning to the basics and gaining a deeper understanding of yourself and your interests. It's possible that upon reflection, you may discover something unexpected about yourself. If you wish to take it a step further, I recommend an additional activity:

Draw an image of yourself in the centre of a page and surround it with words or phrases that represent who you are.

This seemingly simple and innocent activity, often done by children, can be remarkably helpful. Visualising something that symbolises you makes it easier to recognise and appreciate your true likes and preferences, which may otherwise go unnoticed or overlooked.

Through this exercise, you may uncover aspects of yourself that aren't immediately obvious. For example, while you may be a passionate fan of cars and devote significant time to that interest, you might also have a hidden enjoyment for crafting that tends to be overlooked. When someone asks about your interests, the primary hobby often comes to mind first, while the others may be momentarily forgotten. It can be beneficial to recognise and acknowledge all the aspects of life that bring you joy. Utilising a visual aid, such as the activity mentioned previously, can assist you in this process.

Romanticising your life means prioritising your own happiness and dedicating time to activities that bring you joy. It's essential to remember that you have the freedom to choose how you spend your time. While using your phone can be a relaxing pastime, consider exploring other activities that you might enjoy even more. For instance, you could listen to music or indulge in your favourite beverage while using your phone to enhance the experience. By discovering what brings you pleasure, you can incorporate more of those activities into your life and romanticise your everyday experiences.

Moreover, when it comes to romanticising your life, it's not just about the external activities; it's also about developing a deeper understanding and care for yourself. Learning how to nurture and love yourself is crucial. While it's wonderful to find happiness in the presence of others, relying solely on external sources for your happiness can be limiting. You are a constant and permanent presence in your own life, and others may come and go. Therefore, it's vital to cultivate self-love and understand what makes you feel loved and fulfilled. Embrace who you are, appreciate your uniqueness, and provide yourself with the love and care that you deserve. After all, you will be spending every single second of your life with yourself, so why not make it a loving and fulfilling journey?

Getting to know yourself will enable you to identify the emotional aspects in life that bring you fulfilment. Becoming aware with this knowledge, you can incorporate it into your life and become the catalyst for your own happiness. Self-love goes beyond mere affirmations in front of a mirror; it involves allowing yourself to experience and acknowledge your emotions and thoughts without judgment. It encompasses making healthier choices to care for your body and well-being, such as going for walks and spending quality time with yourself. Engaging in activities that cater to your needs is the ultimate expression of self-love.

Allocate some dedicated alone time to sit with yourself and go into the depths of who you are. Discover the things that genuinely ignite your passion and reflect upon why you love engaging in those activities. Sometimes, the true reasons may not be immediately obvious. Drawing from my personal experience, I initially recognised my love for fashion, but it wasn't until I delved deeper and reflected on the underlying reasons that I unravelled its true significance. I discovered that my interest with fashion stemmed from my innate creativity and the joy I derived from experimenting and curating unique looks with my existing wardrobe. Once I uncovered this connection to creativity, I actively incorporated creativity into my life, resulting in a more fulfilling and enjoyable experience.

By exploring and understanding the core aspects of yourself, you can uncover hidden passions and desires that contribute to a more authentic and enriching life. Embrace the process of self-discovery, and let it guide you towards a deeper connection with yourself and a greater sense of fulfilment.

I have also incorporated this type of thinking into other areas of my life. I discovered new passions through doing this, such as what I am doing right now: writing this book. I never realised that I absolutely loved writing and wanted to be an author until I started writing my journals and enjoying writing essays for my university course. I questioned why I loved doing those things and noticed that I love writing about topics I am passionate about, which is exactly what I am doing in this book. When we look deeper into ourselves, uncovering the reasons why we love what we do and invest time in understanding who we are as individuals, we can unlock new wisdom about ourselves. In terms of romanticising your life, the ultimate goal is to find happiness within yourself and in life. You want to pursue the things you have always yearned to do. This is why self-discovery is crucial for your journey on this earth. The most significant influence in your life is you. You make the decisions, and you can be the catalyst for your own happiness. You don't need to wait or seek permission to engage in activities that bring you joy or make you feel loved. You don't need to wait for anyone else. It is up to you, and that is something truly magical.

Sometimes, external influences can greatly impact the way you live your life. However, you can find ways to seek inspiration and strive to achieve more, gaining clarity on how you want to live your best life. Finding inspiration will help you set goals to aspire to, both big and small.

Getting Inspired

Let's say you were given a project to create something. You wouldn't immediately have an idea and start right away. Typically, you would begin by seeking inspiration to guide and generate ideas for what you would like to create.

The same principle applies to romanticising your life. If I ask you to start doing it right now, you might feel confused and unsure of how to begin. Some of you may have a few ideas, like the ones you wrote on your list, but you might not know how to proceed beyond that. This is why it's important to find ways to get inspired, as it will make it much easier for you to pursue your dreams.

To start off, you can visualise how you would like your life to be. Visualisation is an excellent source of inspiration because it gives you a clear idea of how you envision your future life. Think about the emotions you want to feel, the experiences you want to have, and what you want to bring into your life. When you have a clear vision of what you want in your future, you know what you need to work towards. Remember, when deciding what you want for your future, be open and avoid discouraging yourself by believing it is impossible or dismissing it as something others might consider silly. Your attitude towards your desires plays a significant role, especially in finding inspiration. A negative mindset can limit your beliefs and make it harder to find inspiration. Contrarily, a positive mindset and focusing on thoughts that make you feel good will make inspiration flow more easily. Embrace positive thoughts about the present moment and encourage yourself for the future. Naturally, ideas will come to you about what you can do to feel good. You may feel motivated and inspired to go for a walk, for example. Conversely, if you were feeling negative, you would likely lack the motivation to do anything.

Nature is known to be a great source of inspiration. If you're seeking ideas on how to make your life more enjoyable and fulfilling, spending time in nature can provide that inspiration. It can also give you insights into what you want to bring into your future. The change of scenery, fresh air, and sensory engagement in nature can help you relax, reduce stress, and gain a fresh perspective. If you've been struggling with mental health issues, stress, or a general feeling of unease, nature can be highly beneficial in alleviating those challenges.

Practicing self-care is also crucial for feeling good and finding inspiration. Taking care of yourself and engaging in activities that bring you joy, not only improve your overall well-being, but also ignite inspiration for the same reasons mentioned earlier. You might even discover activities that you want to incorporate into your life permanently, forming a routine that enhances your quality of life.

Using positive affirmations can also inspire you. By reprogramming your mind with positive thoughts, you can create a new mindset. Here are some examples of affirmations you can say:

- I am feeling fulfilled in my life.

- My present is always bright.
- I am nourished and inspired.

When you consistently repeat these affirmations, you will start believing them and subconsciously feel inspired to align your life with these statements. Suddenly, you may feel compelled to try new things and find the motivation to pursue the activities you've always wanted to do.

You may have noticed that the key to finding inspiration is to feel good. The examples I've provided are all aimed at relieving stress and negativity, allowing you to align with your happier self. It is in this positive state of being that the best ideas and inspiration flow effortlessly. You won't need to force inspiration because your happy self knows what brings you joy and fulfilment. Your optimistic mindset will support and motivate you to pursue your dreams and make positive changes in your life.

By actively cultivating positive thoughts and taking inspired action, you can manifest your desires and create a better quality of life. As you start implementing small, happy changes, the momentum will build, leading to even more ideas and inspiration. These small changes will snowball into significant transformations, and you'll look back and realise how much happier you've become.

It's important to realise and deeply understand that none of your dreams and desires are too big. You'll embark on an inspiring journey to incorporate what you want into your life. Inspiration can be found everywhere, whether it's in people, nature, animals, or through various media channels like television, phones, websites, or books. Pay attention to how ideas make you feel. If something excites or uplifts you, it's a sign that it resonates with you. Don't dismiss ideas as unattainable; instead, welcome them with open arms, as nothing is impossible. The most challenging part of finding inspiration is believing that you can have it. It may require some effort, but if it's something you truly desire, you can make it happen.

Anything is possible

During childhood, life is filled with wonder and limitless possibilities. A child's mind is brimming with boundless potential, and they wholeheartedly believe that anything is possible if they can imagine it. However, as life progresses, children are exposed to the influence of others, and they often learn that there are certain expectations and limitations placed upon them. Some fortunate individuals are encouraged to pursue their dreams and are supported every step of the way. Others may choose a career path based on financial stability and societal approval, leaving behind lingering thoughts of "what if" and wondering if they could have followed their true passions. Sometimes, people find themselves less fulfilled and happy than they had imagined they would be.

This narrative is quite common because many individuals believe that their lives are limited, that not everything is possible for them. They settle for what they perceive as attainable. However, there are countless stories of individuals who have achieved their dreams, even when others deemed it impossible. But why is this the case? Could it be luck? Perhaps. Does being born into wealth increase the odds? Maybe. While these factors can play a role in the ease of attaining one's desires, they are not the sole determinants. The truth is that anything is possible, but because it exists as a dream, it often feels out of reach. That's why we dream of it in the first place. Those who actively pursue their dreams are the ones who have a chance of making them happen. Of course, there may be risks and uncertainties to consider, but unless you make an attempt, you'll never know what could happen.

Achieving your dreams is all about setting the intention that this is what you're going to do and believing in the possibility of it. Along the way, you may encounter hurdles that seem insurmountable, but with persistence, they can be overcome. A hurdle is not the end of the road to your goal unless you choose to give up. Unfortunately, many people feel disheartened or face seemingly impossible situations, leading them to abandon their dreams. However, every step you take towards your desires can be a valuable lesson. Did your business venture not go as planned? Learn from the experience, make adjustments, and start anew. Don't have the financial means to pursue your aspirations? Explore options like saving money or considering a different job that can help you fund your goals. There is always a path that can lead you to where you need to be, even if it involves trial and error. Don't let setbacks deter you, as they are part of the journey towards your dreams. Remember, they say that it's the journey that matters, not just the destination, so find ways to enjoy the process.

If you genuinely want something, you have the power to make it happen. It may not occur as quickly as you'd like, and that can be frustrating. However, you can take small steps towards your goal, such as conducting research and creating an action plan. By doing so, you'll feel a sense of progress and satisfaction. Remember to celebrate even the smallest milestones along the way, as each one brings you closer to your desired destination. You deserve to reward yourself for your efforts, and celebrating achievements can help motivate you to keep going.

What I mentioned earlier may have sounded focused on significant, life-changing goals, but that's not the case at all. This approach applies to all aspects of life, including the simpler things. Often, we overlook the importance of applying the same effort and belief to smaller goals, such as making time for activities we enjoy. The small pleasures in life are just as valuable as the big ones, even though they are often not taken as seriously. However, they have the power to make life more enjoyable.

All you need to do is believe that you are deserving of a fulfilling life and that it is possible for you to experience all the wonderful pleasures life has to offer, regardless of your circumstances. Belief plays a role in the law of attraction. When you emit positive energy and set intentions that you can achieve your desires, opportunities will come your way. Take a moment to revisit the list you created and pay particular attention to the answers you provided at the beginning. Know that the things you want to incorporate into your life are indeed possible, and all your dreams can come true. I want you to truly believe in this possibility.

To make your dreams a reality, it all comes down to yourself. You are the sole person who can take the necessary actions to pursue the things you want to enjoy. Sometimes, a little bit of motivation and inspiration can kickstart your journey towards taking action, and if you pay attention, you'll find signs all around you guiding you towards your desires. If you struggle with believing in the possibility of your desires, positive thinking can be a powerful tool to combat this. It ultimately boils down to your belief in your own capabilities and what you think is achievable in life. Remind yourself that you deserve to live a life that resembles the beautiful dream you envision. Conversely, if you believe the opposite, you're less likely to take any action towards it. Why would anyone attempt something if they don't believe they can succeed? Affirm to yourself that you are worthy of everything you wish for. Embracing positive thoughts will encourage and propel you forward in making the choices you desire.

If you encounter negative thoughts about the things you want to do, such as "I can't do it" or "This is impossible," take a moment to pause and replace them with three positive thoughts that counteract the negativity. For example, tell yourself, "I can do this," "I possess the potential to excel," or "everything is working in my favour." Making this small change will help reprogram your mind to think more positively. Consider the mindset of an athlete stepping onto the track before a race—do you think they tell themselves they can't do it? Highly unlikely. In fact, they visualise themselves winning and use it as a source of motivation to perform better. Your thoughts play a significant role in creating your reality, so it's essential to ensure that your thoughts support you. If they are dragging you down, remember that you have the ability to change them.

You have the power to achieve anything you desire, live the life you envision, and become the person you aspire to be. The only thing that can truly hinder your progress is yourself.

By now, you may have gained a general idea of how you want to live your best life according to your own terms. If you haven't, that's perfectly fine. Many people haven't deeply contemplated this aspect and it can take time to reach a definitive conclusion. Take some time to reflect and discover how you want to live your life. Now, it's crucial to look into our negative habits and address any issues so that we can overcome them and become the best possible version of ourselves.

Doing The "Hard Work"

Let go of your burdens

First and foremost, I want to emphasise that I am not a psychologist, therapist, or doctor. If you are dealing with deep burdens, I strongly recommend seeking professional advice and assistance from a therapist or doctor.

If you feel the need to seek professional help, please know that there is no shame in doing so. Sometimes we require support from others, and that is nothing to be ashamed of. Personally, therapy has greatly benefited me in my own healing journey. I have learned valuable techniques that helped me process challenging situations and aided in my personal growth.

One of the most significant lessons I've learned, particularly in recent times, is the importance of letting go of what no longer serves you. However, I must acknowledge that letting go is much easier said than done. I realised that I needed to release my past because it no longer defined my present.

The challenge was understanding how to "actually let go" and what it truly meant.

Letting go doesn't imply dismissing or ignoring what happened to you. Rather, it means refraining from allowing it to have a negative influence on your life and embracing the present. Initially, when I attempted to let go of my difficult past, I simply acknowledged what had happened and tried to move forward. While I made some progress, I still found myself dwelling on the events, replaying them in my mind, and contemplating what could have been done differently. It was through journaling and deep introspection that I discovered the true essence of letting go.

For me, letting go meant forgiveness. You may have noticed earlier that when I discussed the challenges I faced, I expressed forgiveness even when ill intentions were directed towards me. However, forgiveness doesn't solely pertain to forgiving others for their actions, as certain circumstances may make it undeserved. Equally important is forgiving oneself and the situation at hand.

I noticed that the experiences of being bullied as a child had a profound impact on my self-esteem. It made me highly anxious and concerned about how others perceived me, especially when meeting new people. Initially, I tried to cope with it by accepting that it had happened, but I found myself constantly dwelling on it. I attempted to regain control by taking precautions to ensure it wouldn't occur again. However, this approach indicated that I hadn't truly dealt with the past, as it continued to influence my actions.

Eventually, I had a realisation. I took the time to reflect on my emotions and how the bullying made me feel. I recognised that trying to control future events was almost impossible and not the answer. Instead, I focused on what I had learned from the experience: I had survived it and emerged with a stronger sense of self-esteem. I came to understand that the opinions of others were not as important as my own happiness. With this newfound perspective, I fully accepted that it had happened to me, yet I no longer gave it any power over my thoughts. I simply started living my life on my own terms.

Crucially, I reached a point of forgiveness. I forgave the situation itself for occurring, acknowledging that it was beyond my control. I also forgave myself for the way I had dealt with it at the time, understanding that I did the best I could with the resources I had. Now, I am at peace with it all. Occasionally, fleeting thoughts about the past may arise, but I allow them to exist without attaching any significance to them, and they naturally fade away.

By going through this process of reflection, acceptance, and forgiveness, I have been able to release the negative impact of those experiences and move forward with a greater sense of freedom and self-assurance.

You might question the need to forgive yourself, thinking, "Why should I forgive myself? It wasn't my fault." And you're absolutely right. It's important not to punish yourself or dwell on the situation you've been through. Instead, forgiveness for yourself is about letting go of any self-blame or harsh judgment. It involves being kind to yourself and acknowledging that you may have been hard on yourself or wished you had acted differently. Forgiveness in this context is about releasing those burdens and offering yourself understanding and compassion.

Equally important is forgiving the situation itself. This means accepting that it happened, recognising the pain it caused, and acknowledging that it may have taught you valuable lessons. We'll go deeper into these lessons later on.

I personally believe that acceptance and forgiveness are interconnected. Acceptance involves acknowledging the reality of what occurred, while forgiveness is about freeing yourself from the weight of that experience. By embracing acceptance and forgiveness, you open the door to eventually moving on and experiencing a greater sense of lightness and freedom.

While beliefs vary from person to person, I hold the belief that everything happens for a reason, even the hardships. I view challenges as opportunities for growth and learning. This perspective resonates with many religious teachings, where stories in sacred texts impart lessons that we can apply to our own lives. Similarly, in films or books, there often exists a moral or lesson that we can learn and incorporate into our own journeys.

By adopting a mindset of learning from every experience, you can find meaning and purpose even in the toughest of circumstances, allowing them to shape you positively and guide your path forward.

Take a moment to reflect on a difficult time you've experienced in the past. Consider how you were as a person during that period. Were you timid, shy, carefree, or hot-tempered? Now, shift your focus to the present and observe how you have changed. Perhaps you've become more confident, speak your mind, or exhibit greater patience. If you're having trouble identifying changes within yourself, try to think about something you have learned from that challenging situation. Initially, this shift in perspective may feel unfamiliar, but with practice and the aid of journaling.

I discovered how much my experiences have shaped me into the strong, independent person I am today. You can do this too.

Another helpful activity is to start journaling and reflect on your day. What events took place today? Did you engage in any activities? After documenting your day's occurrences, whether they were dramatic or part of your usual routine, write down something you learned from the day.

Remember, there's always a lesson to be learned no matter how small. It doesn't have to be a life-changing revelation; it could be as simple as discovering a new approach to a task, engaging in an interesting conversation, or stumbling upon something intriguing on TV. The purpose of this activity is to reprogram your mind to see the bigger picture of situations in your life and gain a fresh perspective.

By practicing these exercises, you can cultivate a mindset that embraces personal growth, learn from every experience, and finds value in even the smallest lessons.

By engaging in these practices, you'll undergo a transformative process of shedding your old skin and embracing a new version of yourself. As time goes on, you'll likely feel lighter and more at peace. In the later chapters of the book, I will go deeper into these topics. After forgiving and recognising how my experiences have shaped me, along with the lessons I've learned, I discovered the power of gratitude. Gratitude has had a profound impact on my life.

Initially, it may be challenging to find things to be grateful for in difficult situations. It might even feel impossible at the moment. However, practicing gratitude doesn't mean labelling the negative events as good. Instead, it helps you find the silver lining and propels you forward. Let's explore some examples of what you can be grateful for:

- I am grateful for the strength and resilience I've developed.

- I am grateful for the courage to stand up for myself.

- I am grateful for the ability to empathise with others.

Remember, cultivating gratitude is a process that takes time. It didn't happen overnight for me, but the journey was undoubtedly worth it. By letting go of past misfortunes, you'll free yourself to focus on the positive aspects of life. There is so much goodness around us, but sometimes our minds become so consumed by negativity that we fail to see it. It's important to remember that what you've experienced is not your fault; difficult times can happen to anyone.

During my journey of dealing with personal issues, one of the most impactful techniques I learned was mindfulness and the practice of being fully present in the moment. This practice has its roots in ancient Eastern and Buddhist philosophy, dating back thousands of years. However, it has gained widespread popularity in Western cultures and has become a global practice, especially in modern times.

Many of us tend to get caught up in our thoughts, constantly overthinking and spiralling into negative mental states. I can certainly admit that I've spent countless hours trapped in the whirlpool of my own thoughts, creating unnecessary stress and anxiety. This became a significant challenge for me, particularly when I was dealing with anxiety. I found myself excessively dwelling on worst-case scenarios and, as a result, avoiding certain activities out of fear. In doing so, I lost touch with the present moment and developed a habit of assuming the worst about everything and everyone around me.

Through the practice of mindfulness, I was able to slow down, observe my thoughts and feelings without judgment, and reconnect with the present moment. It allowed me to simply "be" and appreciate the beauty and peacefulness of life. I must emphasise that I am not perfect; as a human being, I still have moments of overthinking, and I allow myself to experience sadness and release my emotions when needed. What has changed is that I now have the ability to observe my emotional state, acknowledge it without identifying myself solely with that emotion, and remind myself that it is temporary. I reassure myself that the sadness will pass, and I will be okay again.

Mindfulness has been a powerful tool in regaining control over my thoughts and finding inner peace. It takes practice and patience, but the benefits are truly transformative.

Mindfulness is all about being fully present in the moment and, when it comes to our thoughts, simply observing them as if they were clouds. It also involves noticing our surroundings, including what we can hear, smell, and see, as well as any sensations we feel in our bodies. By practicing mindfulness, we can allow ourselves to observe the stream of thoughts that enter our minds, acknowledge them, and let them pass. This practice helps us become more present with ourselves and the world around us, enabling us to truly enjoy life's experiences.

The reason I am highlighting mindfulness is because it compliments romanticism. Romanticism emphasises being in the present moment and deriving joy from it, particularly in the simple aspects of life. Mindfulness aligns with this philosophy by encouraging us to be fully present and observe the present moment.

Incorporating mindfulness into your life can help you perceive things as they are, without judgment or attachment. Additionally, engaging in healing methods can assist you in making the most out of life and experiencing a sense of fulfilment.

To cultivate abundance in life, it is essential to identify and address any detrimental habits we may have, such as overthinking. By finding effective strategies to overcome these habits, we can embark on a journey toward becoming our best selves.

Changing your bad habits

When it comes to recognising and changing our bad habits, it's often difficult to identify them unless someone points them out to us, or we find ourselves in a challenging situation that prompts self-reflection. Figuring out how to overcome these habits can be a frustrating process.

However, this chapter is not about providing a comprehensive list of your bad habits or prescribing specific solutions. Only you can truly understand and address your own habits, whether it's by eliminating them or making adjustments. This guide aims to help you become aware of them and assess if they are hindering you from living life on your own terms or, in this context, from romanticising your life.

It's important to recognise that everyone has a "shadow self," a part of them that embodies negative aspects that can impact both themselves and others. There is no need to feel ashamed about this, as every individual on this planet is imperfect. As we journey through life, we continually learn, grow, and acquire both positive and negative habits. Sometimes, we become aware of our own issues and strive to overcome them. If you find yourself in this position, it demonstrates personal growth and a desire to do what's best for yourself.

When it comes to "overcoming" our bad habits, it's important to acknowledge that not every negative aspect of ourselves can be instantly eliminated. Some habits may persist throughout our lives. However, what we can do is learn to embrace those parts, live with them, and adapt so that they either benefit us or no longer hold us back. Let me provide you with some examples of my own bad habits, which you may relate to and struggle with as well. This way, you can hopefully realise that there's nothing to be ashamed of.

Personally, I struggle with overthinking, attempting to control things beyond my control, and having a fear of the unknown. These issues are connected and stem from my anxiety. They are my anxiety's way of trying to make me feel more secure, but instead, they have caused me difficulties. I have come to accept that these habits are a part of me, and what I do now is focus on what I can control in a situation, such as the present moment and my reactions to it. Mindfulness, as mentioned earlier, has been helpful for me in this regard. If you share similar challenges, incorporating mindfulness into your life might also be beneficial, although everyone's experience and needs are unique, so you may find alternative approaches that work for you.

It is also valuable to explore the root causes of our bad habits. Sometimes, they can be traced back to troubled experiences in our childhood, which have led to certain issues as our minds attempt to cope. For example, someone who constantly brags about their achievements may come across as annoying and self-centred to others. However, what might be unknown is that this person brags because they have self-esteem issues. Perhaps as a child, the only way they received attention and love from their parents was through their achievements. Therefore, they continue to do so in order to feel valued. To overcome this habit, they would need to realise that they are worthy of love and acceptance just as they are, without the need to constantly showcase their accomplishments to everyone. It would involve letting go of the past, forgiving their parents and themselves, and taking action to overcome their bad habit.

Understanding the origins of our habits and addressing them with self-compassion and proactive measures is crucial for personal growth and positive change.

This method can be applied to any situation, and we can try it right now. Think of one of your bad habits that you would like to change. Reflect on where it originated and why you engage in it. If possible, consider any connections it may have to your childhood experiences (if nothing comes to mind, that's alright). Once you have gained insights into its roots, it's time to let go of any associated hurt and allow yourself to feel any emotions that arise from this realisation. Then, forgive yourself and any others who may have been involved.

After going through this process, focus on identifying how you can support yourself in addressing the issue that led to the bad habit. This could involve challenges such as self-doubt, paranoia, or low self-esteem. To help overcome the bad habit, seek out healthy strategies for managing your underlying issues. You can consult with a medical professional like a therapist or explore various online resources.

It's important to note that this method is typically most effective for habits that are relatively easier to overcome, particularly actions we exhibit towards others. However, there may be instances where we struggle on our own and require assistance to conquer these challenges. In such cases, don't hesitate to reach out for support from loved ones who can help you recognise when you're engaging in your bad habit, as often we are unaware of it until it's too late. If you find the process too difficult to tackle by yourself, remember that there are professionals available who can provide guidance and assistance.

Another helpful tip for breaking out of a bad habit is to reward yourself whenever you successfully avoid or stop engaging in that habit. The choice of reward is personal, as it depends on what each individual finds motivating. It could be something materialistic, like a small treat or a meaningful item, or it could be something simple, such as self-praise and acknowledgment.

When you catch yourself in the act of the bad habit and manage to stop it, or when you proactively prevent yourself from engaging in it, having a positive reward can effectively train your brain to associate positive outcomes with not indulging in the habit. This reinforcement helps you break free from the habit over time.

Think of it as training a dog. When teaching a dog a new trick, you provide a reward when it successfully performs the action or even attempts it. This creates an association in the dog's mind between the new action and something rewarding, encouraging the dog to continue doing it. You can apply the same principle to breaking a bad habit in yourself. By consistently rewarding yourself for avoiding the habit, you reinforce the positive behaviour and make it more likely to stick.

So, where does all of this fit into romanticising your life, you may ask?

Romanticising your life ultimately revolves around finding happiness and living your life to its fullest potential. However, before we can dive into the exciting aspects that bring us joy, there's often a need to do some "dirty work" and give ourselves a clean slate. Just like you can't decorate a house and make it beautiful without first clearing away clutter and dirt, the same principle applies here. There might be certain things holding you back from moving forward and fully embracing a romanticised life.

For example, you might be a people pleaser, living your life in a way that you think will make you accepted by others. However, deep down, you may not feel truly happy because of this. Overcoming the habit of people pleasing, gaining confidence in yourself, and living life on your own terms, regardless of what others say, is essential.

Now that you have an understanding of identifying and working on your bad habits, it's time to make an effort to overcome them. By doing so, you'll be cleaning the slate and paving the way for the real magic to unfold. Remember to seek professional help if you feel you need it, as these methods are what have worked for me, but everyone is unique, and there may be other approaches that resonate with you.

Believe in yourself and know that anything you desire is attainable. Have faith in your abilities and take action. This reality is yours, and you have the power to choose how you want to live it. Believe in yourself. Let's also assess your surroundings to determine if they have a positive or negative influence on you, and then find strategies to protect your energy and remain unaffected during tough moments.

Outside influences

All of your surroundings can shape you into who you are because they quite literally define the area you are in, and you naturally adapt to them, whether you realise it or not. The amount of positive and negative energy you encounter on a daily basis can have a significant impact on you. It's important to understand how these surroundings can affect you and take steps to minimise their influence. This can involve cutting out toxic influences and learning techniques to avoid absorbing negativity.

The connection between outside influences and romanticising your life lies in the pursuit of living your best life. If the environment or the people around you are bringing you down, it's essential to find ways to uplift your spirits and create a life that brings you happiness and abundance. While you can't always avoid negativity, there are always options available to help you manage it and make your life a little less stressful.

In this chapter, we will explore different sections to cover the various aspects that can influence your life. We will break them down to understand how each influence can have both positive and negative effects on you. Additionally, we will look into recognising these influences in your own life and, finally, explore what you can do to bring about positive change, should you decide to make any adjustments. The following sections will be covered:

- People
- Social media
- Home
- Career

Section 1: People

The people who surround you have a significant impact on your life, including your relationships, friends, family, colleagues, and anyone else you encounter. Typically, the closer you are to a person, the greater their influence on you. Their attitudes and behaviours can rub off on you, affecting your own emotions and outlook.

For instance, let's consider someone you spend a lot of time with who is positive, cheerful, and funny. Their positivity can have a similar effect on you, making you feel happier and more energised. Conversely, being around someone who is negative, pessimistic, or doubtful can be draining and leave you feeling tired. We can act as beacons when it comes to absorbing energies. Surrounding yourself with positive individuals can uplift and make you feel good, while being surrounded by negative people can leave you feeling depleted and dreading your interactions with them.

If you identify as an empath or an empathic person, you may be even more susceptible to absorbing these energies.

"An empath is a person highly attuned to the feelings and emotions of those around them. Empaths feel what another person is feeling at a deep emotional level." (Campbell, 2022)

For empathic individuals, it becomes especially crucial to surround themselves with people who radiate positive energy in order to uplift their own energy. You may notice that being in the company of positive individuals brightens your day, lightens your mood, and fosters a sense of optimism. These people can recharge you and increase your overall energy levels. On the other hand, being around negative individuals can leave you feeling tired, sad, heavy, stressed, and pessimistic, as if your energy has been drained.

It's important to remember that it's not the fault of the other person when you experience these contrasting effects. Sometimes, compatibility issues arise, and it doesn't mean either of you is a bad person. There will be people with whom you simply don't mesh well, and that's okay. We can't expect to get along perfectly with every individual on this planet, as we are all unique, possess different viewpoints, and come from diverse backgrounds.

When it comes to your workplace, the people you work with can greatly influence your overall job satisfaction. If you don't have a good rapport with your boss, or if they are strict and frequently raise their voice, it can make your work experience more challenging and increase your stress levels. On the other hand, having a supportive, patient, and communicative boss whom you get along with tends to make your work experience more pleasant. I will go further into this topic in the career section of this chapter.

The impact of relationships extends to your educational journey as well, whether you're in school, college, or university. The quality of your relationships with teachers/lecturers and fellow students can significantly influence your educational experience.

In your family life, the dynamics and connections you have with your parents, caregivers, and siblings also play a crucial role. A strong and positive bond can have a good impact on you, while a strained relationship can have the opposite effect. The people you live with, both currently and in the past, contribute to shaping the person you are today. Their presence can also affect your mood in the present moment. For instance, if there is anger in your household, you may sense an intense and uncomfortable atmosphere. Conversely, if someone is in a cheerful mood, it can create a pleasant environment at home.

If you were raised by parents or caregivers who exhibited negative thinking or a pessimistic outlook, you may find that their attitudes impact your own mood and mindset. You might even notice that you've adopted these characteristics as a result of being influenced by those around you. On the other hand, positive attributes displayed by these individuals can inspire you to cultivate a more positive outlook. However, it's important to recognise that other factors also contribute to shaping who you are.

Relationships and friendships are no exception to the influence they have on our lives. As time passes and we become more familiar with someone, spending more time together, we may discover that we aren't always compatible in certain situations, leading to tension and even toxicity. It's important to acknowledge that we don't always encounter the best people for ourselves, and this can result in challenging dynamics and even encounters with individuals who actively make life difficult, such as bullies.

Toxic connections can form without us realising it, and they can bring out our worst qualities. These connections can leave us feeling invalidated, unheard, hurt, uneasy, or angry. The incompatibility may stem from differences in upbringing, opposing beliefs, contrasting life experiences, or conflicting perspectives on reality. Each person has their own version of reality, which they believe to be true. There are numerous other reasons why people may not get along.

It's crucial to recognise toxic relationships and take steps to address or distance ourselves from them. Surrounding ourselves with individuals who uplift, support, and bring out the best in us is key to living a more fulfilling and positive life.

It is crucial to be mindful of how the connections in your life impact you emotionally. Take the time to reflect on your interactions with individuals and assess how they make you feel. Pay attention to the positivity or negativity you experience after spending time with them. It's important to remember that nobody is perfect, and everyone has moments when they may feel down. It's natural to experience a range of emotions in any relationship. What truly matters is how you navigate those emotions and the overall impact the connection has on your well-being.

Keep in mind that individuals may also be going through personal challenges or mental health issues that affect their behaviour. Use your discernment to understand if someone is going through a difficult time, communicate openly, and be considerate of their needs without compromising your own emotional well-being.

Unfortunately, there may be individuals in your life who consistently drain your energy. You may find yourself dreading interactions with them. If you believe that someone is toxic to you, it may be beneficial to reduce or eliminate contact with them if it negatively impacts your life. It can be challenging to do so due to our own conscience and the pressure to maintain certain relationships. We may struggle to prioritise ourselves and fall into the trap of people-pleasing. It's important to recognise and set boundaries with individuals who intentionally try to hurt you. Ultimately, the decision to cut ties or limit contact should be based on what you feel is best for your own well-being and personal connection with that person.

It's true that we may have people in our lives who exhibit negative behaviour or constantly complain, which can be challenging and impact our well-being. However, cutting them out of your life isn't always the only solution. Sometimes, these individuals may be lovely overall and have a strong connection with you, but it's their negative moments that you struggle with.

If you find yourself feeling drained or overwhelmed by someone's negativity, it's important not to feel guilty. As I mentioned earlier, we absorb the energy around us, and being exposed to constant negativity can affect us. It doesn't mean you have to automatically sever the connection. Instead, consider having a calm conversation with them to express how their behaviour makes you feel. Approach the conversation with empathy and understanding, and avoid accusing them, as it may escalate the situation. You can also try helping them see the positives in their situation.

Additionally, there are strategies you can employ to protect your own energy and maintain a sense of grounding. We will explore these techniques later in the book, providing you with tools to safeguard your well-being while navigating such relationships. Remember, each situation is unique, and finding a balance between maintaining a connection and prioritising your own emotional well-being is key.

Section 2: social media

In today's day and age, social media has become an integral part of our lives, whether we admit it or not. It has its positive and negative aspects, just like anything else. The great thing about social media is that you have more control over the influences that surround you. You can choose the type of content you want to see by following specific people and pages. There are many pages that focus on positivity, such as daily motivational quotes, cute animals, and content related to your interests. Following loved ones can also bring some positivity into your feed. You can adjust the algorithms to show you content that you want to see, by engaging with that specific content.

However, there are also pages and accounts that spread negativity, such as constant complaining or sharing bad news. Being exposed to such content in abundance can be stressful and detrimental to your well-being. Additionally, following influencers who seem to have perfect lives and live your dream lifestyle can sometimes have a negative impact. You may find yourself subconsciously comparing your life to theirs, leading to feelings of inadequacy, jealousy, or a sense of lack. It's important to remember that people on social media usually only share the best and most beautiful aspects of their lives.

Another aspect of social media is interacting with other users. It can be a great platform for connecting with people from different cultures, forming communities based on shared interests, and making new friends. However, alongside the positive interactions, you may also come across negative individuals who try to put others down. They may spread hate comments and attempt to belittle people. Encountering such negativity can be upsetting. Fortunately, there are actions you can take, such as blocking these individuals, to limit their impact on your social media experience.

Overall, social media offers both opportunities and challenges. It's essential to be mindful of how you engage with it and to prioritise your emotional well-being by curating your content, setting boundaries, and taking steps to mitigate the negative aspects that may arise.

When using social media, it's important to create a positive and inspiring environment for yourself. The next time you log onto an app or site, approach it mindfully. As you scroll through posts, ask yourself if each one brings you positivity or negativity. Take a closer look at the profile and decide whether you want to follow that account. You can also actively search for profiles that you know will bring you joy and value, ensuring that each time you use social media, you encounter content that uplifts you.

Similarly, consider the people who are following you. Review the list and determine if you are comfortable with everyone seeing the aspects of your life that you share. Being mindful of your followers allows you to maintain a positive online presence and avoid any potential negativity.

Always be conscious of how social media makes you feel. If you consistently come away from it feeling positive, then you've created a positive space for yourself. However, if you find that you don't feel anything or feel negative after using social media, it's a good time to review your feed, remove any sources of negativity, and consider following pages that bring you joy.

Remember, you have control over the content you consume and the people you interact with on social media. Use that control to curate a positive and uplifting experience that aligns with your well-being.

Section 3: Home

The space you live in is where you will likely spend most of your time, apart from your workplace. It is a place where you can relax, find peace, and draw inspiration. Your home can also have an impact on your mood. According to Very well Mind,

"Clutter can increase stress levels, make it difficult to focus" (Susman, 2022)

A clean space, on the other hand, will promote relaxation and a sense of calm. As you may have gathered from the theme of this chapter, your home can shape who you are and significantly impact your mood. If you aspire to live a romanticised and fulfilling life, it is crucial for your house to reflect your true self, bringing you happiness and inspiration. Personally, I find great joy in home decorating! I love exploring antique shops in search of unique pieces that evoke feelings of joy. Every purchase I make is with the intention of adorning my home with objects that ignite wonder and excitement. If something captures my enthusiasm and I can envision its place in my home, I am likely to buy it. I frequently seek online inspiration to discover my decorating preferences. Incorporating elements that engage my senses, such as soft and fluffy materials like blankets and pillows, is important to me. I also take pleasure in candles that emit scents reminiscent of baked goods, as these aromas create a warm and cosy ambiance. My living spaces are curated to evoke relaxation while also providing inspiration. You will find an abundance of nature-inspired and aesthetically pleasing objects in my home. The goal is to create an environment that instils a sense of contentment the moment you step into a room.

If your house brings you joy and a sense of home, you will naturally feel happier in general. There are simple ways to make your home an enjoyable place to be, such as having activities and the opportunity to listen to music out loud. You don't need the most architecturally stunning house, and it's common to encounter problems within your living space. However, there are always actions you can take to refresh your environment, like giving it a thorough clean, decluttering, and rearranging furniture. Every now and then, you can also add items that bring you pleasure. Your home life is important, and the people you share your space with can have an impact on you. Differing opinions on household management can create additional stress, so it's essential to find ways to bring harmony, at least for yourself. Creating a sanctuary where you can escape when things get tough can be beneficial.

If you're dissatisfied with the appearance of your home, it can affect your overall happiness. Coming home after a long day may leave you feeling like you can't fully relax. Your home should be a place where you feel happy and enjoy the space you live in. While redecorating fully may not always be possible due to financial constraints or other reasons, there are small and simple changes you can make to your space. Even if you only have a bedroom or dorm, changing your duvet cover or adding nice pillows can make a difference. Personalise your space with decorations that reflect your taste. It's often the simplest items that can bring about significant changes. By acquiring one new item every month, your space can transform over time. Decluttering is another effective way to change the atmosphere of a room. Imagine having a space filled only with things you absolutely love and that bring you happiness! Additionally, repurposing items and giving them a new decorative twist can make them even more cherished. It's a creative and cost-effective way to breathe new life into objects you already own. It's a win-win situation!

Having a routine in your home life can have a significant impact on your overall well-being. Starting the day on a positive and empowered note can set the tone for the rest of your day. You may experience increased productivity and find your day to be more enjoyable than usual. Contrarily, if you begin the day feeling sluggish, it can lead to a lack of motivation and affect your mood throughout the day.

If you'd like to improve your morning routine and embrace a more romanticised and fulfilling life, you can make small changes that make a big difference. Take a look at your list of aspirations and find inspiration on how to enhance your morning routine. It doesn't have to be complicated. For example, instead of rushing to eat breakfast on the sofa while scrolling through your phone, you can create a simple yet meaningful experience. Slow down and have breakfast at a dining table or outside in your garden if the weather permits. While enjoying your meal, you can listen to a podcast or uplifting music that motivates you for the day ahead. If you feel like engaging in an activity, consider reading a book or watching something that brings you joy. Rather than endlessly scrolling through social media on your phone, opt for a relaxing activity that improves your quality of life.

The choices we make within our homes can shape our lives in significant ways. Opting for activities that physically uplift us and bring joy, rather than mindlessly scrolling through our phones, can have a profound impact on our well-being. Consider swapping out one hour of phone time for a different activity and observe how you feel afterward. You may find yourself feeling more accomplished and fulfilled.

Creating a positive and enjoyable environment at home involves engaging in activities you love, including your hobbies. It's crucial to prioritise activities that bring you joy and help you unwind. Watching movies or series, reading books, or playing video games can be excellent ways to relax and indulge in your interests. Even when you have to do necessary tasks like cooking or chores, you can make them more enjoyable by finding ways to incorporate elements that you love. This book later on also covers strategies for making these activities more enjoyable.

Pay attention to how you genuinely feel in your home and identify what brings you joy and what doesn't. Strive to find a balance that includes activities you enjoy, relaxation time, and strategies to make less enjoyable tasks more pleasant. It's essential to create an environment that nurtures your well-being. If you experience negative emotions related to your living situation, explore possible actions or adaptations that can improve it. Even small improvements can significantly enhance your quality of life.

Section 4: Career

We spend a significant amount of our lives working for a living, starting from a young age and continuing until retirement. Given the time we invest in our work, it's ideal to ensure that our job is enjoyable and feels like a paid hobby. Unfortunately, not everyone has the luxury of finding such a job, but there are ways to make the work experience more enjoyable. The career we choose has a profound impact on our lives and how we live them. This can be influenced by factors such as working hours and the people we interact with, which can have positive or negative effects. The impact is subjective and varies depending on the nature of our work. What truly matters is that the positives outweigh the negatives, and we find ways to cope with and address the challenges that arise.

When we consider the positive ways in which your job can impact you, there are some aspects that may not have crossed your mind. Firstly, your job has the potential to help you find or embody your life's purpose. If you feel that what you do aligns with your true calling, you can create a meaningful impact on the people around you. This sense of achievement can leave you feeling deeply fulfilled. Moreover, this feeling is likely to extend beyond the workplace and permeate your entire day, enabling you to live with a greater sense of fulfilment and happiness. On the other hand, even if you don't currently feel fulfilled in your job, it can serve as a catalyst for self-discovery and lead you to find your true calling. I experienced this firsthand when I worked in a job I disliked, which ultimately helped me realise what I truly wanted from life. Engaging in work you love can generate a sense of motivation and inspiration that carries over into other aspects of your life. At the end of a workday, you may find yourself experiencing a genuine sense of accomplishment, leaving you with a positive outlook.

Another important aspect of your career is the people you interact with, including your co-workers and potential friendships you can form. The presence of enjoyable company in the workplace can have a positive influence on your life. Engaging with supportive and uplifting individuals can leave you feeling energised and uplifted. However, it is also important to acknowledge that there may be instances where you encounter individuals who have a negative impact on your mood or have unpleasant experiences. While it may not always be possible to avoid such situations, later chapters in this book will provide techniques to help you protect your energy and navigate stressful work situations. Since we spend a significant amount of time working, it is crucial to find ways to make it an enjoyable experience.

In the grand scheme of things, every aspect of life shapes who we are and has the potential to impact the way we live. To live your best life, it is important to develop strategies for dealing with negativity, as it is an inevitable part of life. Here are some approaches you can take to navigate these challenges effectively.

First and foremost, practicing mindfulness in the present moment is essential. Stay attuned to your emotions and be aware of any signs of stress, negativity, or a departure from your usual self. Recognising these early indicators enables you to take steps to remove yourself from situations that trigger such feelings, whenever possible. Developing emotional awareness empowers you to take action promptly, whether it's engaging in deep breathing exercises, engaging in a pleasant distraction, or indulging in activities you love. Moreover, extending mindfulness to limit your exposure to negativity is beneficial. For instance, if morning rush-hour travel tends to stress you out, consider leaving home earlier and incorporating enjoyable activities like breakfast at a café before reaching your destination, or a walk in the park near your office.

Another significant factor in your well-being is your thought patterns. Pay attention to whether your thoughts lean toward the positive or negative spectrum. When you catch yourself entertaining negative thoughts, consciously replace them with three positive thoughts instead. For instance, if you find yourself dwelling on how terrible your day has been, counteract it by reminding yourself of the positive aspects of your day or brainstorming ideas to turn it around. By bringing awareness to negative thoughts and actively shifting them toward the positive, you can significantly improve the ease and quality of your life.

Making adjustments to your surroundings and the spaces where you spend your time can be instrumental in protecting your energy. Find a place that brings you joy—a personal retreat where you can seek solace when you're not feeling your best. This place can be anywhere, whether it's within the confines of your home or outdoors. Many suggest that when you're feeling stressed, you should close your eyes and mentally transport yourself to your happy place. Visualise a location that evokes feelings of happiness, safety, and relaxation. This mental escape can provide a much-needed break from the stress of the moment and replenish your energy.

Additionally, consider creating a dedicated space within your home—a sanctuary tailored to your preferences. Fill it with comforting elements such as pillows, blankets, candles, incense, and items that inspire you or bring you joy. Display your favourite photos and include activities that engage your senses. Having a designated safe space to retreat to when you're feeling down can help rejuvenate your spirit and uplift your mood.

Remember to keep this space decluttered, as items can hold energy, and a cluttered environment can disrupt your energetic flow. Extend your decluttering efforts to your clothes, phone, cupboards, and other areas in your life. By reducing clutter, you'll effectively reduce stress, refresh your energy, and create a harmonious and inviting home.

Establishing personal boundaries is crucial for protecting your energy and well-being. At times, people may ask for favours or make requests that you're not comfortable with. It can be challenging to say no, fearing disappointment or conflict. However, politely declining and setting boundaries by saying no to things that don't align with your desires can prevent you from becoming drained and overburdened. Consider the consequences of repeatedly saying yes to things you don't want to do. While there may be instances where you unexpectedly enjoy such experiences, if you anticipate stress or unhappiness, prioritise your own needs by confidently declining. Remember, your well-being takes precedence.

Surround yourself with individuals who uplift and support you. Choose to spend time with co-workers, peers, and friends who bring positivity into your life. Engage in activities with people you genuinely enjoy being around. When you're in the company of those who resonate positively with you, you'll feel energised and inspired. It's important to preserve your own energy and avoid giving too much of it away to others. You're not obligated to assist others if you don't have the necessary energy. Remember, taking care of yourself doesn't make you a bad person—it benefits your overall well-being and contributes to feeling better in the long run.

Spending time outdoors in nature is a wonderful way to recharge and uplift yourself when you feel energetically or emotionally drained. Nature has a profound impact on your mind, emotions, and physical well-being, providing a cleansing and revitalising experience. Additionally, taking deep breaths during moments of stress can help you relax and find grounding in the present. Personally, I've discovered that deep breathing effectively calms me down during anxiety attacks, allowing me to regain a sense of stability.

Harnessing the power of positive words and affirmations can also transform your mindset. By using loving and uplifting self-talk, you can cultivate a sense of well-being and self-love. During challenging times, you can reassure yourself and replace negative thoughts with positive affirmations. Words hold immense power and can be instrumental in shifting your perspective after encountering negativity in your life.

Another effective technique for safeguarding your energy, especially when anticipating encounters with negative situations or people, is visualising yourself within a protective bubble. To do this, begin by taking deep breaths to relax and imagine a radiant golden bubble surrounding you. Visualise it as an impenetrable shield that shields you from external influences. Inside this bubble, imagine a serene and peaceful energy enveloping you. This visualisation technique is widely used and can provide a sense of security throughout your day. Whenever you face challenging situations, you can revisit this practice, ensuring you genuinely feel the presence of the protective bubble and experience deep relaxation.

Once you've acquired the skills to navigate negative situations and interactions, you'll find greater contentment in life, and they won't impact you as profoundly as they once did. Additionally, incorporating positive elements into your life will enhance your enjoyment and enable you to embrace it to the fullest. It's important to acknowledge that perfection and constant happiness are not realistic expectations. However, learning how to improve your well-being in challenging circumstances by expressing your emotions and engaging in activities that uplift you can greatly enhance your life.

Discovering what truly matters to you and aligning your life accordingly empowers you to make necessary changes and take proactive steps toward living your best life. It's a journey of self-discovery that can bring happiness, inspiration, and fulfilment to your existence. By identifying your desires and aspirations, you create opportunities for growth and open doors to a more fulfilling future. Remember, your life is in your hands, and by taking intentional action, you can manifest a life that resonates with your truest self.

Figuring out what you want in life

Hopefully, you are getting into the flow of this and forming some ideas on how you would like to start romanticising your life. Perhaps you have even taken some steps towards that (if not, that's okay, as we will be diving further into it very soon). When we plan to make changes in our lives, it's important to set intentions or goals for what we want to achieve in the long run. Without clear intentions, it can be challenging to figure out where exactly to start or even where we want to go with this.

Firstly, let's focus on identifying what exactly you want to romanticise in your life. I touched upon this topic in Chapter 5, but if you haven't thought about it yet, now is the perfect time to do so. My intentions are to find joy in the simple things, be fully present in each moment, approach life with positive intentions, and pursue my passions.

The question "What do you want in life?" can be overwhelming because it encompasses all the big and small opportunities you'd like to experience. However, to keep things simple, we will specifically focus on the small things that we desire. I'll guide you through a short exercise to help you with this. Just remember, while we're focusing on the small things for now, you can later apply this method to bigger life goals and aspirations in your own time.

Grab a pen and paper, and if you have space on the list you made that is tucked-in this book's pages, that's great. Otherwise, feel free to use another sheet of paper or a journal. Make sure to keep your answers, as they will be helpful for future reference. Whenever you're ready, simply answer the following questions.

1. *What brings you joy?*
2. *What brings you peace?*
3. *What are you passionate about?*
4. *What do you wish your life has more of?*
5. *What would you do if there were no limitations?*
6. *Who do you admire in this world?*

These questions should have been relatively easy to answer. They focused on your enjoyment and exploring possibilities to bring more romanticism into your life. Now, let's go deeper into the reasons behind your answers. This will give you a better understanding of what you truly want and how it can benefit you. Once you have a clear view of your answers, you can start implementing them into your life.

First, let's discuss what brings you joy in more detail. The purpose of this question is simple: to introduce more joy into your life. It's safe to assume that anyone would want to incorporate more joy into their lives, and this question will help you identify what brings you that joy. Seeing your answers written down on paper can often provide a valuable perspective. From there, you can decide whether you want to incorporate more of those things from your list into your life.

Understanding what brings you peace is crucial. Peaceful moments in your life help relieve stress and promote relaxation. These moments can be incredibly enjoyable. It's important to find a balance in your life that includes activities that help you unwind after stressful moments. Some people may mistakenly think that peaceful means boring, but that's far from the truth. There are many peaceful activities that can be fun and enjoyable, such as reading, practicing yoga, or going for a walk. The key is to find what brings you peace and make it personal to you.

Now, let's move on to the next question, which is perhaps the most important one: What are you passionate about? Passion is what drives the world forward. Inventions and breakthroughs have been made because individuals were passionate about what they do. If you can identify your passion, incorporating it into your life will bring you immense joy. It could be a career path or a hobby. If you already know what you love, keep pursuing it with all your heart!

Sometimes, it can be challenging to incorporate things into your life that you wish were already there. There can be various reasons for this, such as lacking a valid reason to do it or facing limitations in terms of money or time. It's important to recognise that these boundaries exist for most people; otherwise, they would already have what they desire. However, just because there are limitations doesn't mean it's impossible to achieve. There may be compromises you can make to pursue your desires and find happiness. For example, if you want to travel but have financial and time constraints, you can explore new places in your local area to experience a sense of adventure while saving up for overseas travel. It may not be exactly what you initially envisioned, but it allows you to do what you want eventually.

Now, let's move on to the next question, which asks what you would do if there were no limitations. This question encourages you to think on a grander scale. Previously, you knew what you wanted to do but felt it wasn't possible. This question prompts you to consider possibilities that you may not have thought of before simply because you believed they were unattainable. Contemplating these possibilities can open up new doors to bring you joy. While some items on your list may not be achievable at the present moment, you can still create compromises and find alternative ways to incorporate elements of your desires into your life, as discussed earlier.

The final question asks about the people you admire in this world. It's important not to compare your life to theirs, as it can lead to feelings of discontent. However, we admire others for a reason, usually because they possess qualities or have experiences that we would like to incorporate into our own lives. For example, you may admire someone who is always helping others. Identifying someone you admire can serve as inspiration to find elements you would like to integrate into your own life, which can bring you happiness. It's a process of trial and error, and you won't know what truly makes you happy until you try it. If you can't directly replicate what someone does, you can always find compromises or adapt their qualities to fit your circumstances.

Now that you have a better understanding of how to bring joy and purpose into your life, let's explore ways to implement them. You might feel confused about how to do this, as you may assume that if you already knew how, you would have done it by now. However, remember that self-discovery and personal growth are ongoing journeys, and it's never too late to make positive changes.

The truth is that while there may be obstacles and challenges that could hinder you from pursuing your desires, there are always alternatives and ways to get started. It may require adaptability and a willingness to explore different paths, but if you truly want something, you will be willing to take the necessary steps. Embracing the belief that anything is possible is a powerful mindset that can propel you forward in the world. Consider this: would the most successful people have achieved their current status if they hadn't believed in themselves and their aspirations? The answer is likely no. They may have encountered significant hurdles along the way, but what sets them apart is their refusal to give up or accept being stuck in their circumstances.

If you find yourself having a mindset that limits your belief in what's possible, don't worry. It's a common mindset that can be influenced by various factors such as upbringing or environment. From this point forward, I encourage you to adopt the belief that anything is possible. This will require some "reprogramming" of your mind, as certain thought patterns may be deeply ingrained in your subconscious, making them difficult to recognise. However, with willpower and determination, it is possible to change this mindset. One effective method is to use affirmations. It's best to personalise them to suit your specific needs, but here are some examples to get you started:

- I am worthy of all my desires.
- I can do and achieve anything I dream of.
- I am the creator of my world.

You should limit the number of affirmations to a small amount, such as 1-3, to ensure simplicity and memorability. The ones I mentioned are quite generalised, but you can personalise them according to your needs. Consider affirmations that reflect what you want in life, such as:

- I live a peaceful and joyful life.
- My life is filled with excitement and abundant opportunities.
- I experience happiness in all aspects of my life and manifest my desires.

These affirmations can be powerful tools to reinforce positive beliefs and align your mindset with your goals. Remember to choose affirmations that resonate with you personally and feel authentic.

When you begin reciting these affirmations, you may experience some self-doubt or discomfort because your subconscious mind might hold opposing beliefs. To overcome this, you can approach it with a mindset of "playing pretend," similar to how a child engages in imaginative play. By fully embodying the affirmations and suspending disbelief, your subconscious mind won't resist them, as there is no perceived risk. This concept is often referred to as "fake it until you make it," and it has been shown to be effective.

An interesting study conducted by psychologist James Laird supports this idea. In his research on self-perception theory, he discovered that participants experienced emotions such as happiness by deliberately smiling, even when they weren't initially feeling happy. Likewise, clenching their teeth led to a sense of anger. Laird's findings emphasise the connection between our physical expressions and emotional experiences.

By applying this principle to affirmations, you can begin to shift your subconscious beliefs and gradually align them with your desired emotions and experiences. Remember that consistency and persistence are key in reprogramming your mindset.

This can also be applied to other scenarios as well. Personally, I have found that feeling anxious about doing something often stems from a lack of confidence in myself. In those moments, I started telling myself affirmations that I was confident and capable. I would count down from 5 and approach the task as if I had no choice, and surprisingly, I found myself feeling more confident and empowered as I took action. This approach can also be applied when practicing affirmations. Over time, you will begin to truly believe in the words you say to yourself.

Once you have figured out what you want in your life, as well as what you do not want, taking action becomes crucial. Negative beliefs can sometimes hinder us from taking the necessary steps towards achieving our dreams. Letting go of these beliefs can be challenging, but it's only difficult if we convince ourselves that it is. Let's overcome this challenge together and show ourselves that we can make positive changes. In the long run, you will look back and be grateful for taking action to transform your life, as it will greatly enhance its quality compared to simply remaining where you were before. Now that we have done the "dirty work," we can introduce positive concepts that will guide us towards becoming our best selves.

Live Your Best Life Now

Having gratitude

Let's begin with what we already have. Often, we tend to take the simplest things for granted because we are so accustomed to them that they fade into the background of our awareness. You've probably heard about the importance of gratitude, especially for essentials like food, water, and shelter. Many families express their gratitude through grace or giving thanks before meals. However, there are also less obvious things that we overlook because they are always present. The trees, the sound of birds chirping, flowers in bloom, the beauty of music, or a sunny day. I make a conscious effort to notice these things regularly. Sometimes, I take solitary walks in silence, fully immersing myself in the surroundings, engaging all my senses, and appreciating each element with gratitude. I find this activity to be incredibly grounding and it strengthens my connection to nature.

As a bonus, this practice aligns with mindfulness, which I mentioned previously. It involves being fully present in the moment and deeply connected to your surroundings. Another powerful way to cultivate gratitude is to imagine your life without someone or something that you cherish. Take a moment to envision your life without that person or pet. Then, consider all the positive qualities they bring into your life. Can you now imagine life without them? It's in these moments of contemplating their absence that we realise how much we truly appreciate their presence. Sometimes, we fail to fully value and appreciate something or someone until they are no longer part of our lives.

Now, let's extend this practice to something broader. Try to imagine a world without the presence of trees, animals, plants, and the sun. Unless you live in a completely urban environment devoid of nature, it is incredibly difficult to imagine such a world. But if we try, we can envision how dull and lifeless it would be. Cultivating gratitude for the elements that surround us is an excellent starting point because, in all likelihood, these things will remain somewhat consistent in our lives. Moreover, it is a quick and easy exercise to recognise the goodness around us. You can try it right now by going to a window and observing what is happening outside.

What do you see, hear, and smell that brings you joy? It could be as simple as feeling the air, basking in the warmth of the sun, or listening to the soothing sound of rain. Take a moment to genuinely feel gratitude for these experiences. Can you imagine a world without them?

If you find it challenging to identify anything outside your window to be grateful for, perhaps you can try this activity the next time you venture out somewhere. You might discover that by engaging in this practice, you begin to appreciate and enjoy the little things that you previously overlooked. Sometimes, we need to encounter things that don't bring us joy in order to fully appreciate the abundance of goodness that is in our lives. Consider this: while many people prefer sunny weather over rainy days, we must recognise that rain is an essential element for nurturing growth and sustaining life on our planet. In this way, even the less favourable aspects of life can contribute to our ability to appreciate and cherish the good. It is a mindset worth cultivating when faced with difficulties.

Practicing gratitude can have a profound emotional impact, especially when done consistently. It can be as simple as waking up in the morning and naming at least three things you are truly grateful for. To take it a step further, you can strive to cultivate gratitude for everything. At first, this may seem like a daunting task, but gratitude is essentially about saying "thank you" and genuinely meaning it. The key lies in the feeling behind the words, as anyone can easily utter the words "thank you," but truly feeling thankful elevates the experience to a whole new level.

When I was younger and learning to say "please" and "thank you," it often felt like a chore, an extra thing to remember to say to people. Perhaps for some people, it still feels that way today. Or maybe it has become a habit, something we do without much thought simply because it's considered good manners. However, saying "thank you" should actually make us feel happy because it's an expression of our appreciation for something in our lives.

Now, I want you to think back to a time when a good happened or you received something that made you genuinely happy, and when you said "thank you," you truly meant it. Take a moment to recall the emotions you felt when expressing your gratitude. I assume it made you feel warm and joyful.

As you cultivate the habit of feeling these positive emotions when you say "thank you" for everything, even the small things, you'll start to experience genuine gratitude. It doesn't have to be an overwhelming surge of emotion; even a subtle wave of happiness is enough. This practice will help you adopt a positive mindset and live in the present moment.

As you cultivate gratitude and practice mindfulness, you will begin to notice the beauty that surrounds you. The simplest things in life will bring you joy because you are consciously aware of the gratitude you hold for them. Whether it's the gentle breeze on your face, the vibrant colours of nature, or the laughter of loved ones, these experiences will become sources of joy and appreciation. By nurturing a grateful mindset, you open yourself up to a world filled with beauty and wonder, enhancing your overall sense of happiness and fulfilment.

In this book, I will also discuss the Law of Attraction because it aligns well with the idea of seeing the beauty in life, living up to your fullest potential, and finding happiness. The Law of Attraction can even bring forth numerous joyous opportunities in your life. While the focus of this book is on romanticising your life, you can harness the power of the Law of Attraction to manifest things or scenarios that help you romanticise the small moments in life.

For me, the Law of Attraction has been the cornerstone of my journey and is something I continuously practice mindfully to my advantage. It has taught me how to find joy in the small things and elevate my vibration. Gratitude is also an integral part of manifesting with the Law of Attraction since it raises your vibration and introduces activities into your life that bring you joy.

Law of Attraction

Funnily enough, when I talk to people who are interested in what I have to share on this topic, I always start off with the Law of Attraction. In the 21st century, it has become much more well-known, so I can only assume that you may have heard of it. If not, let me explain.

According to 'Very Well Mind', it is *a "philosophy suggesting that positive thoughts bring positive results into a person's life, while negative thoughts bring negative outcomes".* (Scott PHD, 2020)

This is a very brief summary; however, the Law of Attraction runs much deeper than that. It is related to the energy or 'vibrations' we emit and is one of the universal laws among many others (I highly recommend looking up the top 12 if it interests you). The Law of Attraction suggests that like attracts like in terms of energy. If you focus on positive feelings, thoughts, and emotions, you attract more positivity into your reality, and the same goes for negativity. It can be a challenging concept to grasp initially, but a commonly used example is to think back to a day when you woke up and something bad happened, causing you to feel grumpy, frustrated, or negative in some way. As you continue with your day, more negative events seem to occur, leading to further negative reactions, whether expressed physically through actions like shouting or mentally through thoughts of frustration. The day ends up becoming a series of unfortunate events, resulting in a bad day for you. This serves as an example of the Law of Attraction working to your disadvantage.

The same principle applies to having a good day. If you wake up in a positive mood, it usually sets the tone for a day filled with good things happening to you.

There are numerous ways to harness the power of the Law of Attraction for manifestation. People employ various techniques to help them achieve their desires. I could write an entire book on this topic! Some of these techniques include affirmations, gratitude practices, mood boards, and scripting. Many individuals incorporate these practices into their morning and bedtime routines to begin and end their days with positive intentions. The possibilities for manifestation are endless, and there is a range of methods that work for different people, although they may not all work for you. It requires some experimentation to find the techniques that resonate with you and yield favourable results.

Personally, my primary method of manifestation involves using music. I have curated playlists featuring songs that evoke the emotions associated with my desired manifestations. For instance, if I want to improve my love life, I listen to upbeat love songs that make me dance, feel happy, and truly experience the emotions of being in love. Every morning, I select a playlist I have previously created and spend 15-30 minutes dancing and immersing myself in those positive emotions. You can use this technique to cultivate specific emotions for the day or attract something particular into your life. It is one of the techniques that consistently brings me great success. Moreover, it is an activity that adds a romanticised touch to my life and brings me immense joy throughout the day.

I will be featuring several techniques that incorporate the Law of Attraction. However, it's worth noting that even if you feel sceptical about it, implementing these techniques into your life can still benefit you by bringing happiness and positivity. In theory, you have nothing to lose. The key aspect is that these practices should be exciting and enjoyable for you. If you're familiar with manifesting, you might have come across methods like scripting and writing out your desires, which may feel like chores to some people. I believe that manifesting should be something that brings you joy rather than a burdensome task. When you engage in these practices with excitement and enjoyment, you're likely to experience better results. By infusing positive energy into the process and genuinely enjoying yourself, you set the stage for manifesting your desires effectively.

Two of my other favourite manifestation techniques are scripting and the 5x55 method, both of which involve writing. The 5x55 method is particularly helpful for quickly manifesting short-term goals, such as attracting money.

To practice this method, grab a sheet of paper or a journal and write out an affirmation of your desire as if you already have it, such as "I received £200" or "I won the lottery." Repeat this affirmation 55 times and do this for five consecutive days. It's crucial to cultivate the feeling that you already possess your desire. By aligning your energy with the frequency of abundance, the 5x55 method helps reprogram your mind and shift you into an abundant mindset. If you find this process tedious, you can make it an enjoyable experience by doing it at night, accompanied by music and a candle. Personalise it to make it something you genuinely enjoy.

Scripting, on the other hand, is a technique I use for manifesting long-term desires like my dream house or dream job. This method is fun because it allows you to unleash your imagination and write down all your wildest dreams as if you already have them. You can write in the form of a letter, as if you are describing your life to someone else. Include vivid descriptions of your desires, engaging all five senses. Feel the emotions you would experience if you were already living your desires. By writing down everything you want as if you already have it, you align your vibration with the manifestation of those desires. Scripting not only helps attract your dreams into reality but also sets you on the path to achieving them. It can be an immensely enjoyable experience, as it allows you to envision and feel the fulfilment of your dreams. You can also incorporate the techniques mentioned earlier to make this process even more enjoyable for you.

Writing may not be everyone's preferred method, but there are plenty of other ways to make manifesting work for you and bring you joy. If you enjoy painting, you can create art that represents the things you love and desire. Take a walk in nature and talk about your desires as if you already have them. The key is to align yourself with the feeling of already having your desires fulfilled. Live your life as your dream self and make choices based on that ideal version of yourself, including your clothing, food, and daily routines. Manifestation and the Law of Attraction encompass much more than these basics, but they serve as a foundation you can incorporate into your life to enhance its romanticism.

So, how does the Law of Attraction fit in with romanticising your life? One of the goals of romanticism is to find enjoyment in more aspects of life and truly feel them. By applying some of the manifestation techniques to your daily life, you can experience that joy, and it's even more rewarding if you manifest something in return. Let's consider my example of manifesting with music. Incorporating this practice into my mornings has brought about a high level of positive energy to start my day. It puts me in a great mood, motivates me, and makes me feel like the protagonist of a movie. The best part is that by starting my day with happiness and high vibrations, the rest of my day tends to follow suit, and I notice amazing opportunities presenting themselves. On the other hand, there have been days when I haven't followed this routine— whether due to forgetfulness or busyness—and I've noticed a stark difference in the atmosphere of my day. I feel more tired, less productive, and even experience mood swings. However, when I listen to uplifting, high-vibrational music, I experience a completely different, positive effect. From my personal experience, I believe that how you start your day has a significant impact on its overall tone, productivity, and your mood. It's definitely a habit I recommend to everyone, especially when you wake up feeling tired and groggy. Adjusting your routine to include this practice might initially be a challenge, and you may feel a bit silly at first, but once you start, you'll find it enjoyable and worthwhile. This applies to any new habit you incorporate into romanticising your life, as it may initially feel unfamiliar and different from your usual routine.

Let's begin by making small and simple changes to your life that can bring you greater enjoyment and help you embrace your true, authentic self. These changes may not be monumental, but you'll discover that they have a profound impact on the way you experience and appreciate life's little moments.

Enjoying the small things

To begin our journey, let's start with small steps. We're going to focus on changing your habits, but we want to avoid overwhelming you with drastic changes. I understand that the idea of altering habits can be daunting and require considerable effort. In fact, when I come across those words of "changing habits" in a self-help book, I can't help but let out a sigh myself.

But fear not! I'm here to make the process easy and enjoyable for you. We'll take a gentle approach, ensuring that you can make the switch without feeling frustrated or overwhelmed. It's all about finding a balance that works for you. So, let's embark on this journey together, one step at a time.

We are going to romanticise our lives right now. Let's take a moment to truly indulge in the experience of reading this book. I invite you to pause for a moment and set the mood to make it more enjoyable for yourself. This is all about personal preference and creating the ideal environment for you.

For me, romanticising the act of reading involves immersing myself in classical or 40s/50s music while sipping a hot cup of tea from my favourite cup. I like to snuggle up on my sofa or bed, wrapped in a cosy blanket and wearing comfortable clothes. If the weather is pleasant, I might even choose to read outside in the countryside or at a charming café. In fact, as I write this book, these are the very things I'm doing to enhance my own experience.

Of course, you don't have to follow these exact suggestions. Instead, I encourage you to do whatever makes this reading experience more pleasurable for you. Take a moment now to create your own ideal setting, and when you're ready, we can continue.

How do you feel now? Let's proceed with our journey together.

Each time you pick up this book, I want you to remember to create an enjoyable experience for yourself. It may initially seem unnecessary or extravagant but consider the concept of luxury experiences. They often include delightful details such as beautiful interiors, exquisite packaging, or extra surprises that make them truly special. From a business perspective, it's considered good practice to entice customers by making them feel valued, with the hope that they will return. So why not extend that same level of care to yourself?

By going the extra mile and adding those special touches, you can enhance even the simplest of experiences. It doesn't have to be extravagant unless you want it to be. What truly matters is that you take pleasure in the experience and make it meaningful for yourself. Treat yourself with the same consideration and thoughtfulness and create experiences for yourself that truly matters.

When it comes to living life, it can become quite mundane, and we often fall into the habit of following the same routines. This is especially true as we grow older and find ourselves juggling work, chores, household responsibilities, and the care of our children, if we have them. It's incredibly easy to slip into what is commonly known as "human airplane mode." This is when we become so accustomed to our daily routines that we carry them out without conscious thought. Our daily chores become repetitive and automatic; merely habits we've developed subconsciously. However, this can pose a slight problem when we find ourselves in "airplane mode" even during activities that are meant to be enjoyable.

I used to have a bad habit of falling into this trap. In the past, I would go on daily walks in the countryside, putting on my earphones and immersing myself in music. However, before I knew it, I would find myself back home without much recollection of the walk itself. I couldn't remember the songs I listened to or truly experience the journey. It wasn't because the walk was uneventful or lacked enjoyment; in fact, I take the same routes even now. The issue was that I had entered "airplane mode," mindlessly going through the motions and disconnecting from the present moment.

Recognising this, I made a conscious effort to practice mindfulness during my walks. I didn't want to give up listening to music or podcasts entirely, so I came up with a solution. On my way to my destination, I would indulge in my favourite tunes or podcasts, allowing myself to fully enjoy the experience. However, on the way back, I would pause, be present, and immerse myself in the sounds of my surroundings. This simple shift has brought me immense pleasure during my walks. Every single day, I now notice the wonders of nature, appreciating the true beauty of the world around me. I have delightful interactions with lovely individuals I encounter, and if I'm lucky, I even spot some fascinating animals. The other day, I encountered a mother and baby deer in a field. It's amazing how often we overlook the remarkable things in life that are right in front of us. Sometimes, all it takes is a small nudge to help us realise the depth of these simple pleasures. It's easy to get caught up in our thoughts and lose focus on the present moment, but by cultivating mindfulness, we can truly embrace the richness of each experience.

One way to overcome this tendency is by regularly checking in with yourself. If you're engaged in an activity that is meant to be enjoyable, take a moment to pause and ask yourself, "How am I feeling right now?" If your answer is happiness, then congratulations, you're fully present in that moment. However, if you find yourself unsure or disconnected, it's likely that you've become lost in thought, diverting your focus from the enjoyable activity. The good news is that simply asking yourself this question serves as a self-realisation that you were mentally drifting. This awareness should help bring you back to the present moment. From there, practice mindfulness to maintain your presence and engagement.

Now that you're more aware of your emotions and self when engaging in enjoyable activities, you can truly savour the present and explore ways to enhance the experience with small acts of romanticisation. I can't provide a one-size-fits-all answer to how you should romanticise these moments, as we all have unique preferences and tastes. This is where your personal list comes into play. When you're fully present and aware, you can ask yourself, "How can I make this experience even better for myself?" Be creative and experiment with new things. If something doesn't quite work or bring you joy, that's perfectly fine— it's all part of the learning process to discover what truly brings you enjoyment. Through trial and error, you'll eventually find a few things that hit the spot and enhance the moment, leaving you with a profound sense of enjoyment and a desire to repeat the experience.

It is all so simple; it's just about doing things that you enjoy. And it shouldn't feel like an effort because you will feel fulfilled and excited to do those things again. If you're unsure about how to approach this, please don't worry. Later on, I will provide you with methods and tasks to help you figure out how to romanticise those happy moments in your life. For now, I'm explaining all of this so that when we reach those methods, you'll have an understanding of what I'm referring to. By reading this section, I hope your gears are turning and you're thinking of ways to enhance the experience of the activities you already enjoy.

Half of the challenge lies in finding ways to further romanticise your life with activities you enjoy. It is much simpler to do when it involves things we already enjoy. However, what about romanticising the not-so-fun activities to make them enjoyable, such as household chores?

It may initially seem daunting, especially when you think about a chore that you dread doing, particularly if it's something you have to do every day. The key is to understand why you dislike it and then find a way to make it enjoyable. In my case, it was washing up. I found it boring and reached a point where I dreaded doing it, especially since I didn't have a dishwasher. So, I decided to transform it into a more enjoyable experience. I started listening to music and singing along while doing the dishes, or I would call a friend and use that time as an opportunity to catch up. Now, it's something I look forward to because I can enjoy the activity and even anticipate it.

Previously in this book, I mentioned that my go-to film for inspiration is Snow White and the Seven Dwarfs. In the film, when Snow White did the housework for the dwarfs, she made it fun by singing songs and enjoying herself. She even got the animals involved in helping. Although I can't have a flock of birds assist me with housework, there's nothing stopping me from talking to my dogs and finding creative ways to involve them.

My point is that there are many ways in which we can infuse joy into 'boring' activities, and sometimes the issue is that we don't know how to do it. The best way to overcome this is by finding inspiration. In my case, I found inspiration by watching Snow White and the Seven Dwarfs. I observed how the characters enjoyed what they were doing and then implemented those joyful elements into my own life.

What I want you to do is choose a household chore that you don't enjoy. For this example, let's go with cleaning the bedroom. Now, take a look at your list of enjoyable activities and see if there's anything that can be combined with the chosen chore. If you don't find a suitable match, don't worry. Make a separate list of things you enjoy doing and see if there's any way to combine them with your chosen activity.

For instance, one of the things I enjoy is dancing and being silly. I can easily incorporate this into cleaning my room by playing some music and letting loose while tidying up. It would make the chore more enjoyable for me.

Now, let's say there's an activity you enjoy that can't be directly combined with the chore you've chosen. Take a look at your list and see if any of the activities can be adapted. For example, I love reading, but it's difficult to read and clean at the same time. However, I can adapt this by listening to an audiobook. I still get the pleasure of immersing myself in a good book while being able to clean my room efficiently. It makes the chore easier compared to doing it in silence. Of course, if you prefer silence while doing the chore, that's perfectly fine too. We all have different preferences, and that's what makes life wonderful.

These small changes can indeed bring great pleasure to your life and serve as a wonderful starting point for romanticising your life and finding greater fulfilment. However, I understand that figuring out how to live life in a positive way and truly feel good about yourself can sometimes be challenging. That's why I want to share with you a method to tap into the frequency of love, enabling you to experience love in everything you do.

The frequency of love

You may have heard the phrase "love makes the world go round," which is, in fact, a song by Deon Jackson. It is quite literally true and let me explain how. Everything we have in life is derived from somebody's love and passion for something. Your mobile phone wouldn't have been invented if someone didn't have love and passion for creating it. Every connection we have involves love, and it's not limited to just romantic love; it can also be family or platonic love. Leading a life filled with love can bring happiness and fulfilment. Even the choices we make can be guided by love. Naturally, when you feel love for something, you will experience a sense of well-being.

Feeling love is accompanied by joy, peace, generosity, and compassion, among other positive emotions. This is because your energy vibrates at a higher frequency, making you feel more vibrant. These elevated feelings can truly enhance your life and elevate your state of consciousness. In this state, negativity and unhealthy thought patterns diminish. You'll embrace life more fully, savouring its positive aspects, and feeling a sense of wholeness. You'll frequently experience balance, fulfilment, and other positive emotions, creating harmony within yourself.

Sometimes, entering this state requires a conscious effort, and you may need to practice and train yourself to feel the sensation of love in order to raise your vibration. Fortunately, it's a simple practice. The challenging part is remembering to do it, especially during difficult times. All you have to do is cultivate a feeling of love for things in life. Set the intention each day to feel love, and over time, it will become natural to you. There are various techniques you can incorporate into your life to help you experience the vibration of love more frequently, including gratitude, which is explored in a dedicated chapter.

One approach is to seek the good in every situation. Life doesn't always go according to plan, and it can bring about negative emotions. It's important to allow yourself to feel those unwanted emotions initially and find ways to release them as needed. Keeping them bottled up is unhealthy and won't benefit you in the long run. Once you've released them, you'll notice that your mind feels clearer, providing the perfect opportunity to look for the positives within the negative situation. By doing so, you'll cultivate greater optimism and a better sense of self and life in general. Living without fear becomes possible because you'll know that you have the ability to overcome any challenge, no matter how difficult it may seem.

Another way to cultivate the vibration of love is by taking care of yourself. Your body is your temple, and when you prioritise your well-being, you naturally feel more love for life because your body feels good. Nourish yourself with foods that are beneficial for your body while also indulging in your favourite treats. Engaging in exercise can also boost your happiness by increasing dopamine levels. It can be as simple as going for a walk or participating in a sport you enjoy. During challenging times, it's important to care for yourself and engage in activities that bring you joy and relaxation. Listening to your body's needs will contribute to your overall well-being. Additionally, creating a space in your home that brings you joy can further enhance your feelings of self-care.

One powerful way to feel good and experience love is by being generous and helping others. You can donate money to a charity, volunteer your time, or simply engage in conversation with someone who may be feeling lonely. When you know that you've made a positive impact, you naturally feel good, and you may find yourself experiencing love and compassion towards the cause or person you've helped.

When faced with negativity in your life, it's important not to judge it but instead approach it with compassion. Observe any negativity you may feel and gently release it, replacing it with feelings of love and peace. Keep your focus on the positive aspects of life, cultivating a mindset that embraces love and gratitude.

You can also tap into the emotion of love at any time, on demand. Take a deep breath and allow yourself to feel love. If you need assistance, think of something or someone that evokes feelings of love within you. As you experience this feeling, sit with it, and try to amplify its intensity, if possible. Notice how it uplifts your mood and state of being.

To reinforce this feeling of love, actively seek opportunities to experience it throughout your day. Whether it's appreciating the beauty of flowers or replacing jealousy with love for what you desire, these practices align with the law of attraction. By projecting feelings of love and positivity, you attract more opportunities and experiences that align with those emotions.

Embracing the law of attraction and living in the frequency of love leads to transformative changes in your life. You will feel light, happy, and whole, experiencing a sense of abundance and fulfilment. By vibrating at the frequency of love, you will attract more love and joy into your life.

By implementing these practices, you will truly start to romanticise your life and feel like you're living your best life. You'll develop a genuine love for life itself and learn to appreciate each moment and the positive aspects it brings. Paying attention to the small things will bring you joy and a deeper sense of fulfilment.

Moreover, as you align yourself with love, you'll naturally gravitate towards activities that bring you joy and avoid those that don't resonate with you. You may find that your perspective shifts, allowing you to discover love even in things you once disliked, or you may choose to let go of what no longer serves you.

To live your best life and experience love for everything, it's crucial to be fully present in the current moment. Many people get caught up in thoughts of the past or worries about the future, missing out on the richness of the present moment. By cultivating mindfulness and embracing the now, you can fully immerse yourself in the beauty and love that surrounds you.

Be in the now

The present moment holds the utmost significance in our lives. While it's beneficial to reflect on the past and learn from it, and to set goals for the future, the key is to maintain a balance and not lose sight of the present. The present moment is where we truly exist and experience life.

When we dwell too much on the past or obsess about the future, we miss out on the beauty and opportunities that the present offers. We need to appreciate the here and now, as it is the only reality we directly encounter. The past and the future are experienced through memories and thoughts, but they are not unfolding in the present moment.

Understanding this concept can be challenging, but Eckhart Tolle's book "The Power of Now" provides a profound exploration of this idea. It delves into the significance of being fully present and embracing the power of the present moment.

By shifting our focus to the now, we can cultivate a deeper sense of peace, fulfilment, and love in our lives.

Living in the present moment is important when it comes to romanticising your life. While it's meaningful to make future plans and have aspirations, they shouldn't overshadow the present. Your current life, the one you are living right now, holds the key to experiencing joy and fulfilment.

Making plans for the future can certainly bring excitement, but it's crucial to remember that the true essence of life is found in the present moment. By being fully present and engaged, you can make the most of each moment and create a life that brings you happiness and satisfaction.

Utilising the past and the future can be beneficial in shaping your present. Reflecting on your past experiences can guide you in making choices that align with your preferences and desires. Similarly, envisioning your future can inspire you to take action in the present to work towards your goals.

For instance, if you have a destination in mind for the future, you can start planning and taking steps now to make that a reality.

The key is to strike a balance between appreciating the present moment and harnessing the lessons and inspirations from the past and the future. By embracing the power of the now, you can create a life that is meaningful, joyful, and aligned with your true desires.

To make life a better experience in the present moment, start by tuning in to your feelings and asking yourself how you truly feel. This self-awareness allows you to identify areas that could be improved or enhanced. Once you have that clarity, you can take intentional action to make the current moment even better.

Practicing gratitude and mindfulness are effective ways to shift your focus back to the present moment. Engaging in meditation and deep, intentional breaths can help you centre yourself and cultivate a sense of presence. Additionally, by actively noticing and appreciating the things that surround you, you can engage your senses and find joy in the present.

Slowing down and savouring the simple pleasures of life is a wonderful way to be fully present. Take the time to notice and appreciate the beauty that surrounds you. Find enjoyment in everyday activities by immersing yourself in them wholeheartedly. By embracing life at a slower pace, you will discover a profound appreciation for things you may have overlooked before. Being fully present in the moment brings a sense of peace and allows you to flow with life's natural rhythm.

By incorporating these practices and immersing yourself in the present moment, you will find that life becomes more fulfilling and peaceful. Embrace the beauty of each moment and let yourself be carried by the flow of life.

It's important not to dwell on the past or worry excessively about the future, as neither is happening in the present moment. Liberating yourself from this mindset allows you to make conscious decisions and take action to improve your current situation. You have the power to choose activities that bring you joy and make the most of your goals right now.

Time is indeed precious, and it's common for younger individuals to underestimate its value compared to those who are older. I had a profound realisation of this during a bus ride home from college when I overheard a conversation between two older ladies, perhaps in their 60s or 70s. They spoke about how quickly life had passed and the simple things they wished they had done but were now unable to due to their age. Their list included activities like dancing all night or climbing a specific mountain.

This experience made me reflect on the simple things I had postponed for another day, assuming there would always be time in the future. However, as time passed, I realised that there was always another excuse or delay. Fortunately, being young and in good health, I still have many opportunities ahead of me. If you're reading this and find yourself further along in life, this realisation may resonate with you if there are unfulfilled desires you long to pursue. Remember, it is never too late.

While some limitations may arise due to health issues and age, there is always a way to work around them. It may require creative thinking and a willingness to step outside the box. If there are activities you've put off thinking you could do them anytime, why not try doing them now or in the near future? Perhaps it's baking a cake or visiting a particular place. Embrace the present moment and engage in the things you've always wanted to do. Life is a precious gift, and our time in this lifetime is limited. Live it fully in the present, pursuing your passions and desires. You can even document your aspirations in a diary or take action today. By making an effort to enjoy the present, you can look back with satisfaction and minimal regrets. And if there are any regrets, use that moment of reflection to take action and fulfil your desires.

Overall, we have covered various individual ways and techniques that can help you improve your life. We explored these throughout this chapter and the first part of this book. Now, we will delve into each aspect of your life and examine how you can optimise it to reach its fullest potential. While we briefly touched upon this topic in previous chapters, we will now take a deep dive into it. By the time you reach the end of this book, my aim is for you to feel motivated and inspired to implement meaningful changes that will enable you to thrive in your life.

How To Romanticise Your

Career

Introduction

First and foremost, it's important to acknowledge that achieving the perfect career is an unrealistic expectation. There are numerous variables beyond your control, such as co-workers, bosses, workload, customers, and the overall work environment. Many times, our current job may not align with our dream job or fail to meet our initial expectations. Perhaps you find yourself in a position where you aspire to climb the ladder and attain a higher position. It's worth noting that many successful people such as film directors started from humble beginnings and gradually worked their way up to their desired roles. On the other hand, some individuals may have taken any available job out of sheer necessity to sustain themselves in this world. Life presents countless factors that can affect the quality of our careers. Nevertheless, our goal is to improve your current job situation and potentially inspire you to pursue a new career path if it resonates with you and aligns with your aspirations.

So, what does it mean to romanticise your job? It doesn't involve simply daydreaming at your desk and pretending it's better than it actually is or trying to convince yourself of its greatness. Romanticising your job requires taking action and approaching it from a fresh perspective, making small changes that can improve your experience. It's about infusing your career with renewed enthusiasm and believing in its potential for greatness. In this section, I will provide you with tips and ideas on how you can make the most of your job. While I can offer examples and suggestions, it's ultimately up to you to make the effort and explore new approaches to enhance your job satisfaction. Considering the significant amount of time we spend working, it's crucial to find enjoyment in what we do. Your job can provide you with new experiences, and if you can find ways to maximise its positive aspects and derive joy from it, you'll hopefully discover a sense of fulfilment. In a later chapter of this book, I will provide further guidance on how you can make the most of your current job.

It's important to ensure that any actions you take in your workplace are allowed and align with the rules and regulations in your workplace. Additionally, it's crucial to be mindful of your work performance and understand that every action carries consequences. For instance, if your idea of enjoying your time at work involves doing nothing, the consequence could be disciplinary action or even the risk of losing your job. So, it's essential to exercise mindfulness and make wise choices.

Now, let's delve into strategies for thriving in your career. To begin, it's helpful to reflect on where you currently stand and how you feel about your job. This reflection will provide insight into your current reality and serve as a starting point for identifying areas where you can make improvements. Once you have a clear understanding of your situation, you can explore and determine the specific actions you can take to make the most of your work experience.

Reflecting on your career

Reflection is a valuable practice when it comes to personal growth and making positive changes in our lives. By taking the time to reflect, we can gain clarity on our feelings and identify areas where we can bring about improvements. It's important to conduct regular check-ups on ourselves and honestly evaluate various aspects of our lives.

Now, let's begin by reflecting on your career. Start by focusing on the positives of your job. What aspects do you genuinely love about your work? Take the time to jot down these positive aspects as they can provide you with a sense of direction and help you identify what you want to incorporate more into your work life. For example, if one of the highlights is the people you work with, consider ways to deepen your connections with them. Perhaps you could plan a casual outing, like grabbing a drink together, to get to know them better and foster stronger relationships. Sometimes, it's the simplest tasks or moments that bring us pure joy, so don't overlook them. It could be the pleasure of reading a document, performing a specific task, or even enjoying your lunch break.

Furthermore, think about how you can enhance the positive aspects of your job. Let me share an example: I know someone who works in a highly stressful environment with demanding managers and tight schedules. To facilitate communication and make the job more efficient, the company introduced headsets for staff members to be easily contacted. Surprisingly, this change had an unexpected positive outcome. The staff began interacting more, sharing laughs, and eventually started meeting outside of work for social activities. As a result, their connections grew stronger, and their overall work experience became more enjoyable.

By reflecting on the positives and finding ways to amplify them, you can make your career more fulfilling and create a more enjoyable work environment.

There are always ways to work around a situation and make it much better. Sometimes, it does require thinking outside of the box! Take a moment to consider if you could incorporate more of what you already enjoy into your job. You can take this a step further and examine your list. Look at the things you enjoy doing or want to incorporate more into your life and see if they could be integrated into your work. By doing so, you will hopefully experience greater fulfilment and may even pursue some of your desires.

Now, let's view your job as a whole from a neutral standpoint. Take some time to sit with yourself and realistically assess how your job makes you feel. If you have positive thoughts and emotions, you can always enhance your experience as we discussed previously. However, if you have neutral feelings where you don't love your job but don't hate it either, focusing on incorporating things you enjoy will benefit you the most. Since there are no negative aspects to worry about, you can concentrate on making your experience better.

On the other hand, if the thought of your job leaves you feeling down or drained, filled with negative emotions, it may require more effort to change this. We will look into that shortly. Additionally, consider your career as a whole. Are you currently in your dream job? Do you envision staying in your current job long term? Are you aiming for a promotion? Evaluating your goals and ambitions can help you determine the best course of action in the present moment.

For some individuals, transitioning to a new job could be beneficial. However, for others, it may not significantly change things since certain tasks, like writing emails, may remain regardless of the job. While this might be a tedious aspect for some, it could be just a small part of the job, even if it's their dream job.

Next, it's time to reflect on what you dislike about your job. Take note of these aspects, as they will help you determine what you want to change. Consider whether these dislikes are mandatory for your job and cannot be altered, or if there's a possibility of stopping or modifying them. Once you have identified the areas of improvement, think of ways to make them better. While I can't provide specific solutions for every job, I can encourage you to incorporate elements you love to enhance your tasks. Even simple things like listening to music can make a difference. Reflect on your personal preferences and you may discover ways to improve your overall experience. If you're still unsure about what to do, try searching online for tips on making your job better or specific advice related to your tasks, such as "tips to make writing emails easier." It may require some trial and error, but there's always a solution. Embrace your creativity.

To summarise this chapter, assess your feelings about your job by answering these questions:

- What do you love about your job?

- How can you incorporate more of what you enjoy into it?

- Realistically evaluate how your job makes you feel and consider if you desire any changes, such as pursuing a new job.

- Identify aspects you dislike. Can you stop them? How can you make them better?

Overall, strive to make the most out of your career. Determine what you want to experience and let that inspiration and motivation drive you to take action. Remember, you only have one life, so it's up to you to maximise its potential. Let's explore how you can seize this opportunity and make a positive difference in your work life.

Take action on your career

Achieving your dream job requires taking action and making changes. The same applies to making changes in your life or career. You can't expect things to magically change without putting in the effort. In the previous chapters, you may have identified ideas or changes you want to pursue in your job. However, that's only the first step. Real change occurs when you take action.

In this chapter, we'll explore how to act on your desires and provide prompts to motivate you. You'll also find inspiration to generate ideas and improve your overall experience. Since job types vary greatly, the specific actions you need to take will depend on your unique circumstances. It's understandable if you feel a bit lost or frustrated in figuring out what to do. Trust that if you genuinely want to make a change, ideas will naturally come to you.

Additionally, please be aware that there might be some repetition of ideas mentioned throughout this book. This repetition serves to reinforce these concepts in your mind and remind you of the available options you can explore.

To initiate change, it's important to be open to it and keep your options available. There may be amazing opportunities waiting for you, so it's worth keeping an eye out for new job openings that align with your aspirations. You could explore the possibility of changing positions within your current organisation or even negotiate for a raise. Another option is to consider a career switch or pursue further studies that will ultimately lead to a different job. It's crucial to remember that even if you feel trapped in your current life situation, there are always alternatives available.

Sometimes, all it takes is a change in perspective to make a significant difference. Let's say you have a 30-minute train commute to work, which you typically dislike. Shifting your perspective can completely transform the experience. Start viewing it as an opportunity to relax or engage in activities you enjoy. You can listen to your favourite music, meditations, podcasts, read a book, or even watch a movie during your commute. Personally, I used to dread my 2-hour train rides twice a week, but by changing my perspective, I now look forward to them as valuable free time to indulge in activities I enjoy. Similarly, you can alter your perspective about work by anticipating the opportunity to socialise and engage in activities you're paid for.

Remember, embracing change and adopting a fresh perspective can open doors to greater fulfilment and satisfaction in your career.

To enhance your job satisfaction, it's important to discover ways to make it enjoyable. While simple strategies like listening to music, socialising with colleagues, decorating your workspace, or enjoying delicious food during your lunch break can contribute to a positive work experience, there are numerous other techniques you can employ to make your job more pleasurable and effortless.

One effective approach is to reward yourself each time you accomplish a task. These rewards need not be extravagant; they can be as simple as treating yourself to a snack, taking a brief break, or going for a short walk in the workplace. By doing this, you'll experience a sense of accomplishment and boost your overall mood. If your workload is demanding and stress-inducing, it's essential to explore ways to manage it effectively and increase your productivity. You can utilise productivity apps if you're comfortable with technology or opt for the traditional method of maintaining a to-do list. Breaking down tasks into smaller, more manageable chunks can alleviate pressure and provide a sense of progress and achievement.

By implementing these strategies, you can create a more enjoyable and fulfilling work environment that supports your productivity and overall well-being. Remember, finding personalised approaches that work for you is key to making the most out of your job.

There are many ways to make it enjoyable; it just requires a bit of effort to start off with and change things up a bit to make your work environment interesting. This will make you look forward to the next time you are working. Even the smallest changes can create the biggest impact.

The best part is that you can personalise it to suit you. Just because 'Person A' does something specific to make their job fun doesn't necessarily mean it would be enjoyable for 'Person B' to incorporate it into their work. We all have different personal interests as humans, which opens up numerous opportunities to make your job a little different and special by incorporating what you love. Take a look at the list you previously wrote about how you could romanticise your life. You never know, there may be ways to incorporate some of those ideas into your work life.

Connecting with your co-workers can make all the difference in your work life. If you are a sociable person, this may come naturally to you. For others, it can be a challenge as socialising may require a bit of effort, or some may prefer moments of solitude. If you want to connect more with others while at your job, there are many ways you can do this.

There are different approaches you can take to connect with your co-workers, such as giving compliments. This can actually boost the morale of the workspace and improve the atmosphere of your job because your colleagues will feel appreciated. It doesn't have to be about looks; you could compliment the work they have done or how cute their kid is in a photo. These simple compliments will surely be appreciated.

Making time to hang out with your co-workers outside of work hours can help you build long-lasting friendships. By doing this, you will start feeling excited about going to work because it means you get to see your friends. Initially, meeting up after work may not feel exciting as you might want to escape and feel like your job time is being extended. However, as you hang out, you may find that everyone starts to relax and enjoy themselves. You can go out to lunch or dinner, grab a drink, go for a run, or even commute to and from work together. Start by making a small effort, and you will find that connections will naturally be made.

Sometimes, there are co-workers we don't get along with. In such cases, try your best to focus your energy on the people you enjoy being around. If you have to communicate or work with someone with whom you don't get along, despite your efforts, try to protect your energy. Envision yourself in a protective bubble to create a sense of safety. Sadly, there are times when connections become toxic, and it's best to involve someone in charge of handling such situations. They may be able to make changes, such as reassigning your work area or addressing the other person. Remember, there is always something you can do, even if the situation isn't ideal.

A significant part of ensuring a great workday is starting your day off right. How you wake up and what you choose to do in the morning can greatly impact the rest of your day. Creating a morning routine that works for you and motivates you will benefit your work life. Have you ever noticed that if you wake up feeling groggy, it can set the tone for the rest of the day? You might continue feeling lazy, and the overall mood of your day reflects that. The same applies when you start your day with activities that make you feel good. You'll find more energy and motivation to carry that positivity throughout the day. If you wake up dreading work, it can put you in a not-so-great mood, and by the time you arrive at your workplace, you may feel unmotivated, potentially leading to a bad day. This negative cycle can persist, as a bad day at work can make you dread the next shift, perpetuating the cycle of not enjoying work.

Fortunately, you can change this by establishing a routine to set yourself up for a good day. Find ways to motivate yourself, such as listening to a motivational podcast to get you going. Meditation and exercise can also help with this. Visualising and reminding yourself of your goals can be powerful motivators to propel you towards where you want to be. If you still lack motivation, try faking it until you make it. Pretend that you are genuinely excited to go to work and focus on things that bring you excitement. Embrace the optimism and enthusiasm, and you may find that, without even realising it, you start feeling genuinely excited, leading to a better-than-expected workday. Optimism is the key, and if your day doesn't go as planned, use it as an opportunity to treat yourself to some good food and take care of yourself as a reward. This will hopefully keep you motivated for your next shift because there was still a positive outcome for you.

To enjoy your job more, you can also try to maximise your overall experience. Volunteer for additional tasks or responsibilities in your job, which can lead to extra benefits or at least provide you with more varied experiences to make your job more enjoyable. Consider taking classes or undergoing training to improve and expand your skill set, opening up more opportunities and knowledge in your work. Making the most of your job experience will leave you with a sense of accomplishment in what you do. Remember, life is precious, so why not strive to make the most out of everything you undertake? Additionally, you can organise or participate in activities such as fundraisers or holiday events to add some excitement. It's not always about doing more work to enhance your job experience, but also incorporating fun activities. Moreover, you can express gratitude for what you have. Keep in mind that someone in this world might be desperately seeking a job like yours. Realising this can provide a fresh perspective and help you make the most of your current situation.

To find more ways to enjoy your job, it's crucial to prioritise taking plenty of breaks. Working hard at a constant pace can eventually lead to exhaustion and burnout, draining any enjoyment from your job and making you dread it. Incorporating regular breaks is essential to maintain your energy and prevent burnout. Make it a habit to take breaks while you work, even if you're eager to accomplish tasks. It's vital to value this time for eating, drinking, or simply resting. By doing so, you'll be able to sustain productivity and motivation throughout your shift. If possible, take short breaks during work as well. These breaks don't have to be lengthy; even a 3-5 minute pause after completing a task can refresh you and prepare you for the next one.

Another type of break is when you're not working. Switching off from work can be challenging, particularly for those who are self-employed or work from home. It's important to have moments where you can fully detach from work and focus on other aspects of your life. This allows you to relax and enjoy your personal time without constantly thinking about work. By doing so, when you return to work, you'll feel refreshed and rejuvenated because you didn't spend your free time consumed by work-related thoughts.

Remember that making the most out of your career isn't limited to these points alone. They are merely ideas to inspire you and encourage you to generate your own. It can be challenging to find motivation and have a great, productive day at work. The key is to focus on the aspects that make you feel good. Small things like dressing in a way that makes you feel confident or using a favourite mug can contribute to your happiness while working. Set goals for yourself that will help you strive for the achievements you desire in your career. It's important to have a sense of direction and work towards a bigger purpose, rather than just viewing work as a series of chores. This purpose can be seeking a promotion or simply making the most out of your work to find personal fulfilment and happiness.

Take the time to sit and identify the emotions you want to experience while at work. Then, ask yourself what you can do in your workplace to evoke those emotions. Our desires are often driven by emotions, as we strive to feel a certain way. By determining actions that can elicit those desired emotions, you'll find a sense of joy in what you do.

Overall

Finding ways to feel like you're making the most of your job and finding happiness in your work may require some trial and error. It's important to remember that it's part of the journey. Ultimately, you need to prioritise what makes you truly happy. While earning a substantial income and becoming a millionaire might seem desirable, if the job brings you misery and consumes most of your days, is it truly worth it? If your sole motivation for a job is money, are you really seeking money itself or the emotions and feelings that often accompany financial success, such as freedom and peace of mind? Perhaps there are alternative paths to evoke these emotions. I'm not suggesting that you shouldn't pursue a job for financial reasons, as some may strive for wealth and financial security, while others may simply need a job to meet basic survival needs. However, it's essential to understand your own happiness and pursue what aligns with your values.

Reflect on what brings you genuine happiness and find ways to incorporate it into your current job. Set goals for your life that go beyond material possessions and consider the emotions you want to experience. With time, you can strive for a state of fulfilment in achieving those goals and emotions.

Now that you have ideas on how to improve your job and make the most out of it, remember that this is just one aspect we'll be exploring. The ultimate goal is to live your best life and make the most out of every aspect. Now that we've discussed what you can do with your job, it's up to you to take action. Consider what you love and dislike about your current situation and make changes accordingly. Even small adjustments like decorating your workspace or changing your style can make a difference. Visualise your dream life and imagine how you would live in that way. Then, embody it and become the person you want to be when it comes to your work. Envision your workday in the best possible way, with your ideal scenario in mind. Think about what you would do differently. Once you have an idea, start implementing it. It doesn't have to be perfect or exact, but any small changes will move you forward from where you currently stand. If the change works out, you'll be ahead of where you started. If it doesn't, you can either go back to your original state and try again or explore new alternatives. Though there's a possibility that things may not go according to plan, at least you'll have an understanding of what works and what doesn't. Hopefully, this will set the ball rolling and inspire you to take more steps.

Now that you potentially have an idea of how to romanticise your career to enjoy it, let's explore how you can romanticise your relationships.

How To Romanticise Your

Relationships

Introduction

The relationships we have with others can add a lot of value to our lives. When it comes to romanticising them, it's important to be careful not to overdo it, as this can lead to more problems. The same applies to romanticising anything else – we don't want to dream about something so intensely that we end up feeling disappointed when it doesn't match our reality. Relationships involve two people: you and the other person. Therefore, it's crucial to consider their wants and feelings as well, and keep them in mind when forming connections.

To begin, let me share what you should avoid doing when it comes to romanticising your connections in order to make the most of these relationships. Firstly, refrain from piling all your needs on a person, as you are ultimately responsible for yourself. It's important not to create an idealised image or fantasy of how you want this person to be. Placing them on a pedestal and having unrealistic expectations can lead to disappointment when reality sets in. It might even put unnecessary pressure on them to meet your vision. Another pitfall to avoid is romanticising toxic traits or solely focusing on the positive aspects. Ignoring toxic behaviour or mistreatment will ultimately harm you. At times, we may want to see the best in someone, especially if they treated us well in the past, hoping they will change in the future. However, it's crucial to recognise that sometimes people will not change, and clinging to that belief will only bring you pain in the long run. Reflection on these connections is important to determine your next steps.

When it comes to maximising the value of your connections with others, it's about seeing them for what they are and making simple, healthy changes to fully embrace the positive aspects. Rather than using the term "romanticising connections," let's approach it as making the most of your connections, which essentially means the same thing. There are numerous ways to enhance your connections, fostering deeper bonds and truly appreciating the company of others while getting to know them on a deeper level.

It's crucial to acknowledge that relationships are a two-way street. While someone may appear to be a good match in your perspective, they may not share the same sentiments. If you develop deeper feelings for a friend and view them romantically, it's important to respect their feelings if they don't reciprocate. There may also be instances where someone decides they no longer want you in their life. While this can be painful, it's essential to honour their decision. Instead of worrying, trust that the people who are meant to be in your life will remain, and you will encounter many remarkable individuals along the way.

Now that we've covered the basic idea, let's look into the details of what you should and shouldn't do when it comes to romanticising a connection. Here are a few guidelines to keep in mind:

- Do love and appreciate the person for who they truly are.

- Don't create fantasies about how you want them to be.

- Do express gratitude for their amazing qualities and actions.

- Don't overlook any toxic traits or mistreatment.

- Do communicate openly about your feelings regarding the connection.

- Don't impose unreasonable expectations or try to change them to fit your ideal.

- Do embrace the present moment and enjoy your time together.

- Don't place yourself or your connections on a pedestal; remember that everyone is equal.

As you can see, it's quite straightforward. The key is to remind yourself that romanticising connections doesn't mean pursuing relationships differently. Instead, it involves being mindful and adjusting your mindset to appreciate and make the most out of your connections as they are, without trying to force change or manipulation to fit your desires.

If you're looking to introduce some physical changes in your connection, you can suggest engaging in new activities together. This could involve trying out different hobbies, exploring new places, or embarking on adventures. Additionally, you can diversify your conversation topics to foster deeper connections and gain a better understanding of each other. These small changes can bring about a fresh dynamic in your connection without placing overwhelming expectations on the other person. Remember, the goal is to create shared experiences and open avenues for meaningful interactions.

Finally, it's important to remember that no one else is responsible for your happiness; you must rely on yourself for that. While people can enhance your life and create wonderful memories with you, relying solely on your connections for happiness can lead to problems. You might find that others don't always meet your expectations, causing frustration. Instead, finding happiness within yourself and embracing who you are and what you do allows for greater satisfaction in your present relationships. This goal of feeling whole and not dependent on others for happiness should be your ultimate aim.

Similar to the previous section on romanticising your career, we will now engage in reflection to identify your desires, enabling us to take appropriate actions to maximise the potential of your connections.

Reflecting on your relationships

Understanding your desires and reflecting on your current connections allows you to gain clarity on your position and take necessary action. Similar to the career section, we will assess the strengths and weaknesses of your connections. Additionally, we'll explore the need for establishing personal boundaries and evaluate your satisfaction with the people in your life. Periodically evaluating your relationships is a healthy practice, providing insight into how you feel about those you have formed connections with. You can conduct this assessment by considering your connections collectively or by examining each relationship individually.

Before we proceed, it's important to remember that nobody is perfect, and it's not their responsibility to be perfect for you. If you feel that some of your needs, such as communication or spending more time together, are not being met, you can express these concerns to the person involved. However, it's important to recognise that you cannot force them to change. For instance, they might be too busy to increase the time you spend together. In such cases, it's up to you to take the next step forward. It's possible that you might need to learn how to fulfil these desires on your own. Sometimes, there may be certain emotions you believe can only be satisfied by others. Later in this relationship section of the book, we will explore how you can find a sense of wholeness within yourself. This will enrich your relationships with others because you won't have expectations for them to fill a void.

To begin, take a moment to consider who in your life brings you happiness. This exercise allows you to identify these individuals and cultivate a sense of gratitude towards them. Going further, reflect on the specific aspects of these connections that contribute to your happiness. You may discover that each relationship has its own unique qualities. For example, one friend may excel at engaging conversations and offering valuable advice, while another friend brings humour and joy to new experiences. Everyone is distinct and possesses their own wonderful qualities. It's highly unlikely to find someone who meets all your criteria and possesses every desired quality. That's why it's beneficial to have multiple friends, reducing the pressure to find "the perfect person."

Now let's turn our attention to reflecting on negative connections you may have with others. Some individuals are fortunate to be surrounded by supportive and loving people after setting healthy boundaries. Personally, I count myself among those fortunate few. However, I have encountered my fair share of toxic individuals who had a negative impact on my life. These individuals can exist in the form of friendships, family members, or even romantic partners. Take a moment to reflect on people who could potentially have a negative influence on you. These are the individuals who leave you feeling drained or negative after interacting with them.

Next, consider if there are specific aspects of connections that do not serve you well. This could include engaging in constant conflicts, getting involved in drama and gossip, or dealing with someone who consistently exhibits negative personality traits. By identifying these aspects that you prefer not to experience in your connections, you can establish a starting point for creating boundaries and effectively communicating them.

Now, let's go deeper into reflecting on your relationships. Consider what you would like to experience more in these connections. Instead of focusing on wanting people to change, concentrate on the experiences you desire. Take it a step further and identify any specific emotions you would like to feel. For instance, in a romantic relationship, you may long to feel loved and secure. By pinpointing the emotions you feel are lacking and would like to experience, you can explore ways to cultivate those emotions.

One option is to introduce these emotions into your current connections, but it's essential to communicate openly with the other person as they may not feel comfortable with certain changes, such as introducing romance into a friendship. Another option is to seek out new connections that have the potential to fulfil these desired emotions, such as embarking on dating to find a romantic partner. It's important to note that this may take time.

Lastly, you can cultivate these emotions within yourself, allowing you to feel more fulfilled and satisfied. This independence will foster healthier connections since you won't be dependent on others to fulfil your emotional needs. However, it's crucial to strike a balance. While it's beneficial to be independent and not rely solely on others for happiness and fulfilment, human connections are valuable and can provide support. Finding this balance will allow you to enjoy the benefits of both independence and meaningful connections.

It's crucial to prioritise your own well-being and not allow others to take advantage of your energy. Take the time to reflect and review the boundaries you have set in your relationships to ensure you are being treated with respect. These boundaries can be personal and serve as a guide to determine if people are crossing them.

Once you have reflected on your existing boundaries, consider if there are any additional boundaries you feel you should set. If you have experienced mistreatment in the past, it is important to establish a boundary to ensure you are not subjected to similar treatment again. If someone crosses that boundary, communicate your concerns to them and make it clear that such behaviour is unacceptable.

If the person continues to disregard your boundaries, you may need to take further action in your connection with them, including considering the possibility of cutting them out of your life. Prioritising your own well-being and surrounding yourself with people who respect your boundaries is crucial for maintaining healthy relationships.

To summarise the reflection prompts from this chapter, here are a few questions you can answer and write down your responses. Engaging in this process will allow you to dive deeper into your thoughts and provide a reference point for taking action:

- Who brings you happiness?

- What aspects of your relationships bring you joy?

- Are there any individuals who don't bring you happiness? (If applicable)

- What aspects of your relationships do you not enjoy?

- What do you desire from your relationships?

- Which emotions do you seek to experience in your connections?

- What boundaries have you established with people?

- Are there any boundaries you feel you should set with others?

By reflecting on your current relationships, identifying the positive aspects, and considering the changes or additions you desire, you can use these answers as a foundation for taking proactive steps. Before we delve into strategies for enhancing your connections, let's begin by focusing on your individual journey.

Be your own source of happiness

Making yourself a priority is vital if you want to improve your connections. Your ultimate goal is to find happiness in these relationships, but relying solely on others to provide that happiness can create limitations. When you feel fulfilled and happy on your own, without depending on others, it releases subconscious pressures for them to fulfil a certain role in your life. By letting go of these expectations, you can cultivate a greater sense of gratitude towards the people who are already in your life, appreciating them for who they truly are.

This lesson has been a significant one for me. It wasn't just about my relationships with people; it extended to seeking happiness from external sources. For a long time, I relied on others to be my primary source of happiness. If I found myself alone and not engaged in any activities, I would feel unsatisfied. I attempted to derive satisfaction by constantly talking to and spending time with others. However, this became problematic when those people were unavailable or busy with their own lives, such as work. It led me to believe that I needed more friends and that I was lonely. Through introspection, I came to the realisation that I wasn't truly lonely; I had subconsciously placed expectations on myself, believing that constant interaction with others was necessary for my happiness. To overcome this, I started engaging in activities that brought me joy and learned to appreciate moments of solitude. I began listening to podcasts during quiet times. By fulfilling my own need for constant communication and finding happiness within myself, I was able to cultivate healthier relationships. I now communicate with my friends less frequently, but our conversations are more meaningful. And when someone isn't available to talk, I feel at ease and relaxed about it.

I want you to revisit what you mentioned in the previous chapter when you were asked about what you desire more in your relationships. Take some time to reflect on the emotions you would like to experience within your connections. The reason for this exercise is to encourage you to focus on fulfilling these desires within yourself first. It's likely that if you've identified certain needs or feelings, it's because there's a sense of lack or longing. By addressing these needs internally, it doesn't mean you shouldn't seek them from your connections. You can still pursue these desires with your current relationships or in new ones. However, it's important to recognise that it may not be an instant solution. For instance, wanting a new friend can be challenging since you can never predict when or if you'll meet someone who possesses the specific qualities you seek. With your existing connections, you may choose to communicate your desires, but it's not always guaranteed that the other person will reciprocate those desires.

Fulfilling these needs within yourself will lead to a quicker sense of satisfaction and a healthier perspective on your relationships. Take a moment to identify the needs you wish to fulfil and explore how you can meet them on your own. Keep in mind that some needs may require the involvement of others, particularly if they are specific to certain individuals. For instance, if you desire more communication from someone, it's important to express this to them directly. Take the time to understand why you desire increased communication and look into the underlying emotions. A common example is when casually dating someone and they don't text back frequently. If you develop feelings for them, their lack of communication may trigger feelings of being unwanted or unworthy. In such cases, try to cultivate feelings of self-love, worthiness, and contentment within yourself. This mindset will allow you to go with the flow in your connections, understanding that what is meant to be will unfold naturally. In the mentioned scenario, the person may eventually communicate their feelings for you while explaining their busy schedule, enabling you to decide if you want to pursue a deeper connection. On the other hand, they may abruptly stop communicating without apparent reason. Although it may still sting, you can find solace in knowing your own worth and make a conscious decision to explore new connections or embrace being solo for a while.

Practicing self-care is essential for looking after yourself and meeting your own needs. When you prioritise self-care, you not only nurture your well-being but also establish a blueprint for how you deserve to be treated by others. Taking care of yourself sends a message to the world that you value and respect yourself, and it sets the tone for the kind of treatment you expect from others. By setting healthy boundaries and practicing self-care, you can create an environment where others are less likely to treat you poorly. Remember, your well-being matters, and taking care of yourself is a powerful way to ensure that you are treated with the kindness and respect you deserve.

It's important to find joy in the present moment, even when you're alone and not actively doing anything. By embracing the stillness and simply being with yourself, you can experience a deep sense of fulfilment. This is something I'm still learning myself, but I've noticed that it has a profound impact on all aspects of life, including my relationships with others. When you recognise that external factors are not the sole source of your happiness, you can appreciate them as additional blessings rather than necessities. Of course, there are still moments when the desire for activity arises, and that's completely natural. Remember, we're all human, and this journey towards finding contentment is continuous. Embracing the present and enjoying your own company will undoubtedly enrich your life and enhance your connections with others.

Improving your relationship with yourself is crucial in reducing the pressure to have your needs fulfilled by others. It's important to examine your own behaviour and consider whether you may be unintentionally hurting others or yourself. Breaking free from toxic patterns and behaviours will undoubtedly improve your relationships with others. You may find that people have kept their distance from you due to these negative behaviours, but by actively working on personal growth and positive change, you can create a space for stronger connections to develop. Reflecting on any patterns that may be off-putting to others, such as frequent anger or constant negativity, is essential. Remember that people may distance themselves to protect their own energy. If you recognise toxic traits within yourself, be kind and compassionate. We are all human, and often, these patterns occur without our conscious awareness. By acknowledging and working on personal growth, you can create healthier and more fulfilling connections with others.

Some people may have communicated this to you, and you might have perceived it as nagging or criticism. However, it's important to consider that these individuals may have been trying to engage in open and honest communication because they value your connection and want to express their needs. Showing empathy towards their perspective and finding a compromise, as well as adjusting your own behaviour, can greatly contribute to the growth and success of your relationships. On the other hand, choosing not to take responsibility for this feedback may result in the deterioration of the connection or the distancing of the other person.

Overall, in order for your connections to thrive and for you to make the most out of them, it is essential to prioritise your own well-being. By focusing on your own happiness and not relying solely on relationships to bring you joy, you will experience a sense of liberation and reduce the pressure placed on yourself and others. This newfound empowerment will open up opportunities for personal growth and allow you to explore strategies to cultivate contentment within yourself. In the next chapter, we will go into how you can optimise your positive connections and make the most of them.

Make the most out of your relationships

Your relationships with people will inevitably encounter challenges and imperfections. Sometimes, life gets busy, and we may lose touch with one another. Other times, individuals may be going through personal struggles, causing temporary unavailability. As previously mentioned, it is crucial not to burden others or yourself with unrealistic expectations of having flawless connections. It is perfectly acceptable to take time for yourself when needed, as we are all human and face our own difficulties.

That being said, there are numerous strategies you can employ to maximise the potential of your relationships. By implementing these practices, both parties can thrive and forge even stronger connections. Without further ado, let's delve into these approaches.

First and foremost, effective communication is arguably the cornerstone of any meaningful relationship. It extends beyond mere talking and encompasses active listening as well. Your relationships will greatly benefit from open and honest dialogue with the other person. You can start by asking about your friends' day or checking in on someone you haven't spoken to in a while. Engaging in conversations that go beyond surface-level interactions shows that you value and appreciate them. These discussions can also delve into new and interesting topics, allowing you to discover more about each other. Don't be afraid to ask out-of-the-box questions to spark deeper conversations.

It's important to note that you don't need to communicate every day, as both of you will have other commitments in your lives. However, making an effort to meet up regularly, whether it's once a week, fortnightly, or once a month, can help nurture your connection and allow it to grow. During these encounters, prioritise active listening and genuine engagement with what the other person is saying. It's equally important to ensure that this level of engagement is reciprocated by the other person.

By fostering open communication and active listening, you can cultivate stronger and more fulfilling connections with the people in your life.

Taking your connections further involves truly connecting with each other. It's not enough to engage in shallow communication without the intention of forming a genuine bond. Superficial conversations tend to leave you unsatisfied. To foster thriving connections, invest effort into understanding and connecting with the other person on a deeper level.

Take the opportunity to open up about your passions and what brings you joy. Sharing these aspects of yourself helps build trust and strengthens the bonds between you. It's important to be your authentic self and allow the other person to see the real you. If they genuinely value you, they will appreciate your vulnerability and reciprocate by sharing their authentic self as well.

This authenticity and vulnerability contribute to building trust and create a sense of knowing each other more intimately. It can also make the other person feel valued, knowing that you trust them enough to be your true self.

Building this level of connection takes time, as it's not something you would typically do with someone you've just met. It's important to get to know someone gradually and establish a foundation of trust before going into more personal matters. Once you feel comfortable and trust has been established, you can begin discussing deeper and more personal topics.

By developing authentic connections, being vulnerable, and gradually opening up, you can cultivate deeper and more meaningful relationships with the people in your life.

When you're already deeply connected with someone, it's important to be authentic and vulnerable by letting them in when you're going through a tough time. It's common to worry about burdening others with our struggles, but instead of simply saying you're fine when asked how you are, allow this person to truly know how you're feeling. Open up and let them see all sides of you. It's essential to recognise that they can't fix your problems, and it's important for both of you to understand that. However, being able to share and have them listen can be beneficial for both you and the growth of your connection.

It's crucial not to solely rely on one person when you're facing difficulties. If your struggles become the sole focus of your communication, it can lead to burnout for the other person and potentially create dependency on them for your well-being. Constantly discussing your issues 24/7 with someone is neither enjoyable nor healthy. If you notice that someone you know tends to talk about their problems constantly, try steering the conversation towards other topics after listening for a while. This can be beneficial for both of you, providing a good distraction and allowing for a more balanced and enjoyable conversation.

Being open and honest in your relationships is crucial as it builds trust and prevents problems in the long run. Lying can create a web of complications, as the truth tends to emerge eventually. Trust is especially vital in intimate relationships, as it forms the foundation for growth, strength, and longevity. Strive to be open and honest about anything that involves the other person, even if the truth may be difficult or painful. By doing so, you demonstrate respect and show that you trust them enough to be transparent.

As you begin to trust someone, you can foster that trust by sharing something personal or confidential with them—something that not many others know. If they keep it to themselves and refrain from passing judgment, it can deepen your connection and facilitate further growth. When both individuals in a relationship are authentic, open, and maintain trust, their connections can truly flourish.

It's essential to work on yourself and maintain confidentiality. When someone confides in you, respect their trust by not sharing their secrets with others, even if those individuals are unfamiliar to them. Put yourself in their shoes and consider how you would feel if someone betrayed your confidence by spreading your secrets. Trust is a two-way street, and it's necessary to be reliable and trustworthy in your relationships.

Being there for the people in your life during their difficult times is important. You don't have to dedicate all your time or act as a therapist to solve their problems. Sometimes, a simple invitation to grab a coffee and providing a listening ear can make a significant difference. Be a good listener, validate their emotions, and let them know that you are there to support them. Engaging in activities that bring both of you joy, such as sharing funny stories or discussing shared passions, can also uplift their spirits. These positive moments contribute to being there for each other and foster a strong bond in your connections.

Supporting each other's successes is vital in building strong connections. When your friend or loved one achieves something significant, such as landing their dream job, it's important to celebrate their achievements and share in their joy. By doing so, you demonstrate your support for them and their aspirations. This fosters a sense of trust and openness, making them more likely to share their dreams with you. Celebrating victories together strengthens your connection and brings a sense of fulfilment to both parties.

However, it's important to address any feelings of envy or comparison that may arise when witnessing the achievements of others. Envy can drain your energy and undermine the joy in your connections. Instead of feeling envious, remind yourself that if your loved ones can achieve their dreams, so can you. Shift your perspective to one of excitement for their accomplishments. By raising your own vibration through positive emotions, you attract opportunities for celebration into your own life. Use their achievements as inspiration and affirmation that you too can achieve your dreams.

To maximise your connections, both you and the other person should make an effort to engage in activities together. This can be as simple as scheduling regular phone or video calls to stay connected and hear each other's voices or see each other's faces. Planning to meet up in person is another great way to spend quality time together, whether it's inviting them over for dinner, meeting at a bar or restaurant, or even going on day trips to explore new things. Sharing experiences and creating memories together adds excitement to your connection.

In romantic relationships, it's essential to continue dating your partner, even after settling into a routine. It's easy to become complacent and neglect putting in effort. However, by intentionally planning and going on dates or weekends away, you can inject freshness and keep the relationship vibrant. These shared experiences allow for deeper connections and contribute to the excitement and growth of your relationship.

At the end of the day, you can ensure that you follow the previously mentioned suggestions to make the most out of your connections, keeping them healthy and being the best version of yourself for the other person. However, regardless of the type of connection you have—whether it's family relations, friendships, or relationships—it is crucial to avoid one-sidedness. It becomes unfair when all the effort is being put in by only one party. If you find yourself feeling this way with someone, it may be worth communicating your concerns to them. By doing so, you may discover that they were unaware of the situation and can hopefully make a greater effort going forward. It's possible that they have been preoccupied with personal challenges or simply lacked the time to invest in their connections. Unfortunately, there's also the unfortunate possibility that they don't genuinely care to make an effort. In such cases, it is essential for you to reflect on how you would like to proceed. You might choose to reduce your own effort in the relationship or consider letting go of the connection altogether.

While it is valuable to explore how you can optimise your connections with others, your ultimate priority should be your own happiness and well-being. It is important that the people in your life bring you joy and leave you feeling energised after conversations or encounters. However, it's not always the case that all connections will leave you with positive feelings. There may be instances where certain connections make you feel bad, and the next chapter will delve deeper into this topic. It will explore strategies to navigate these connections and empower you to live your best life.

The bad connections

It may seem like the easiest and most obvious thing to do when you experience a bad connection is to cut them out of your life. While yes, this is a good way to deal with many of these connections and can bring you peace in the end, it isn't always the easiest thing to do. Some people may feel like they don't have a choice in the matter. External factors can also play a role in this decision, as well as the nature of the connection itself, whether it's a friend, boss, or even a parent.

This book has already covered what to do in the case of toxic connections, so this chapter will be brief and provide advice on how to handle them. Firstly, it is useful to be able to identify if you are experiencing a toxic connection. The first tell-tale sign is your emotions. If you constantly feel drained and unhappy when interacting with a person, it is a sign that they are toxic for you. You may feel the need to constantly watch your back around someone who frequently gets angry, fearing that they may snap at you. Additionally, encountering someone with a consistently negative worldview and vocalising it can bring you down and make you feel weighed down by negativity.

Toxicity can manifest in various ways, and the person involved may not even be aware of it. One example is extreme neediness, where they constantly seek your attention and time. Initially, this may feel flattering, as if they want to be around you all the time. However, it can quickly become draining, toxic, and even manipulative. They may not direct their negativity towards you specifically, but their harsh and critical attitude towards others can still impact your well-being. Disrespectful behaviour and unnecessary involvement in their problematic situations can also be red flags.

Checking in with yourself after spending time with someone is important to assess whether they may be toxic. While emotions can serve as a good indicator, it's crucial to ensure that you feel heard, can be your authentic self, uphold your values, and maintain a sense of equality in the relationship. Sometimes, certain individuals can leave us feeling inferior, especially in work environments with hierarchical structures, where those in higher positions may develop a superiority complex that extends beyond their professional role.

It is normal to encounter bumps in the road within your connections, but what truly matters is open and honest communication about your feelings. By expressing yourself, you give the other person an opportunity to understand your perspective, address any issues, and work towards resolution. During these conversations, it is crucial to acknowledge the other person's feelings as well. When sharing your emotions, try using "I" statements to convey how you feel without sounding accusatory. For example, you can say, "I feel this way when you speak like that." This approach allows you to express your emotions without directly confronting or accusing the other person.

Furthermore, it is vital to establish and uphold your boundaries and core values. Don't allow others to cross your boundaries or compromise your values for their sake. Being assertive when expressing your feelings ensures that you are not easily pushed around, particularly by individuals who make you feel small or insignificant. Remember, maintaining your self-respect and assertiveness is key to fostering healthy connections.

When dealing with toxic individuals, it is crucial to safeguard your energy and not allow their words or actions to affect you deeply. This is easier said than done. Remember that any negative comments they make about you do not define your worth. Often, people express their pain and insecurities by trying to bring others down. If someone attempts to assert superiority over you, it is likely because they themselves feel inferior.

Taking care of yourself should always be a priority, and you should never sacrifice your well-being or neglect your own needs for the sake of someone else. You are the main priority in your life, and it is essential to establish healthy boundaries and prioritise self-care.

Avoid rationalising or justifying the toxic behaviour of others. For instance, if a parent has lost their job, it does not excuse them from mistreating you or causing you harm. However, if someone is struggling and exhibiting harmful behaviour, it may be beneficial to communicate with them about how their actions are impacting you. They may not be fully aware of the consequences of their behaviour and addressing it can lead to positive changes in the relationship. Remember, your emotional well-being matters, and it is important to surround yourself with people who uplift and support you.

Once you have identified toxic connections, it is important to decide how you will proceed. In certain situations, it may be best to create distance and remove yourself from these individuals. However, there are instances where this may not be possible, such as dealing with colleagues, neighbours, or family members. In such cases, your focus should be on protecting your energy, prioritising self-care, and making yourself the main priority.

Make an effort to limit your interactions with these individuals as much as possible. When you do have to communicate with them, respond to negativity in a compassionate manner. By doing so, you minimise the chances of giving them ammunition to use against you or provoking retaliation.

After any interaction with a toxic person, practice self-care and engage in aftercare for yourself. Refuse to let their negativity impact the rest of your day. Take time to do something that makes you feel better and replenishes your energy. If someone makes you feel anxious, take steps to relax and calm yourself. Raise your own vibration by engaging in activities that bring positivity into your life and uplift your spirits.

Remember, protecting your energy and well-being is essential. Surround yourself with positive influences and focus on maintaining a healthy and fulfilling life.

We cannot control other people's actions towards us; however, we can make decisions about what we do after a negative interaction. You can find ways to make yourself feel better, so you don't dwell on it all day. It is important to trust your own feelings and decisions regarding how you want to proceed with toxic people in your life. Remember that you and your feelings are a priority.

Overall

We can't idealise our connections and expect them to be exactly how we want because they involve other people. However, we can strive to be the best version of ourselves and make efforts in our connections. The key to finding happiness in our connections is to cultivate happiness within ourselves and fulfil our own needs. When we do this, the rest will naturally fall into place.

Take the time to reflect on who brings joy and positivity into your life, as well as those who bring unhappiness. Engage with people, get to know them on a deeper level, and create shared experiences together. By doing so, you will create wonderful memories to cherish and look back on.

Perhaps you could romanticise your life with someone. You could go on "work dates" and socialise together in an independent café. You could go on mindful walks, inviting that person over to have a drink in your favourite glassware. Hosting a small dinner party and putting effort into making a lovely meal can create an enjoyable evening together. Take a look at the list you wrote a while back and see if there are any activities you can do with a loved one. The best moments in life are usually the ones that are shared.

If, after reading this chapter, you find that you don't have anyone in mind who has a positive impact or close connections, don't worry. You can still apply the points mentioned to deepen your current connections or take the opportunity to put yourself out there and meet new people. One way to do this is by pursuing your passions and engaging in activities or clubs where you can meet like-minded individuals. In today's digital age, social media provides a platform to connect with others and make friends online. However, it's essential to exercise caution when interacting with strangers online, as not everyone may have the best intentions. Nevertheless, I have personally encountered some of the loveliest people online and formed strong connections with them. So, don't hesitate to explore these avenues and open yourself up to new connections.

Now let's look into how you can romanticise your home life and create an environment where you can thrive and feel great. Your home should be a sanctuary that brings you joy and comfort.

How To Romanticise Your

Home Life

Introduction

Home life has a significant impact on our overall well-being and satisfaction in life. Since we spend a substantial amount of time at home, it serves as our sanctuary and refuge from the outside world. It should be a place where we can recharge and prepare ourselves for the next chapter of our lives, whether it involves work or other adventures.

When our home is a source of happiness and comfort, it can replenish our energy and provide a space for self-expression. Coming back to a welcoming and nurturing environment can uplift our spirits and contribute to a positive mindset. On the other hand, if our home life is less than ideal due to various factors such as challenging housemates, an unappealing physical space, or an unfavourable location, it can impact our well-being and leave us feeling less fulfilled.

However, even in less-than-ideal circumstances, we can make the most of what we have. Finding ways to create a positive and personal space within the limitations can make a significant difference. It could involve adding personal touches to the decor, decluttering and organising to create a sense of order, or seeking solace in small moments of peace and tranquillity. Embracing gratitude for the present situation and focusing on the aspects within our control can help us cultivate contentment and make our living space more enjoyable.

Remember, home is not just a physical place but also a state of mind. It's about finding comfort, security, and a sense of belonging wherever we may be. By acknowledging the importance of home life and taking steps to make it a nurturing and fulfilling space, we can enhance the quality of our lives and create a haven that truly feels like our own.

This section aims to provide inspiration and guidance on how to enhance your home life, allowing you to find greater satisfaction in your current living situation and potentially even thrive. Romanticising your home life involves creating a delightful experience, tailored to your personal preferences. There are various aspects you can focus on to infuse romance into your living space, including the surrounding areas, activities, chores, and the individuals (or absence thereof) with whom you share your space. By addressing each key area of your home life, you can cultivate an environment that promotes well-being and encourages a more joyful experience at home.

While there are always aspects of home life we may not enjoy, such as paying household bills and doing chores, for some individuals, challenges may arise from the people they share their house with. Each person's situation is unique, and struggles may differ. Although this book cannot cover every scenario, it aims to offer inspiration that can be adapted and put into action, creating even a small positive difference in your home life.

Everyone deserves to be able to maximise the potential of their home life and create an environment that is as fulfilling as possible. Even if things aren't perfect at the moment, we all have the capability to make changes, whether that means considering a move to a new location or implementing small changes and habits that can enhance our daily lives. We will go deeper into these possibilities later in this section.

To begin, let's explore the physical and design aspects of your home. This encompasses how your home looks, the emotions it evokes, and the steps you can take to make it better, even if it involves focusing on a small area of your home.

Living in a house you love

The appearance of your house can significantly impact your mood. If your living space is decorated in a way that aligns with your taste, it is likely to leave you in a happier state. On the other hand, if your house is dirty, cluttered, or doesn't reflect your personal style, it can leave you feeling tired, uninspired, and in a less-than-ideal mood. Dealing with a mess can be particularly stressful, as it adds an extra task to your already busy schedule.

This challenge can be even more daunting when you share a house, don't own it, or have a strict landlord. In such situations, you may feel limited in your ability to make changes and may have to "put up with" the current state of your living space. If this resonates with your situation, don't worry. This chapter offers inspiration and guidance tailored to address these challenges and help you improve your home life, even within the constraints you may be facing.

One effective way to improve the atmosphere of your space is by decluttering. The items in your house carry energy, and having too many belongings can create a sense of energetic congestion. Every item holds positive, neutral, or negative energy. By creating more physical and energetic space through decluttering, you can cultivate a more uplifting environment. If possible, keep only the things that bring you joy. When you walk into your space, you'll be greeted by items that evoke happiness and positive feelings.

Decluttering not only affects your physical space but also declutters your mind. Being in a space filled with things can overwhelm and cloud your thinking. The presence of numerous items can trigger thoughts of cleaning and maintenance, leading to added stress. By decluttering, you create mental clarity and a sense of calm.

An added benefit of decluttering is that it opens up room for items you genuinely enjoy. You can sell items that no longer bring you joy as second-hand and use the proceeds to purchase something that sparks joy. Whether you choose something new or find a beautiful second-hand piece, you'll be enhancing your space while also minimising waste.

If you find yourself in a situation where you can't declutter the entire house due to factors beyond your control, focus on a specific area that you can have authority over. This could be your own bedroom or a designated space within your room if you share it with others. By concentrating your efforts on a particular area, you can still create a personal sanctuary amidst the rest of the house.

If the rest of the house is in a messy state, you can offer to clean and improve it, making it more pleasant than before. Engage in a conversation with the people you share the house with to discuss possible changes and contribute your input to the decor. When sharing a home, it's essential that everyone has a voice. Each person may have different preferences in terms of decoration, so finding a compromise that accommodates everyone's tastes may be required.

Remember, even small changes and improvements in your immediate surroundings can have a positive impact on your overall well-being and the way you experience your home.

When it comes to transforming your space and seeking a significant change, it's natural to worry about the associated expenses. However, there are ways to achieve this without breaking the bank. One simple yet effective approach is to rearrange your furniture. By rearranging the existing items in your room, you can create a fresh and new perspective that satisfies your aesthetic desires.

If you have a limited budget but still want to add new elements to redecorate your space, you can adopt a gradual approach. Purchase items gradually over time, allowing you to reach a point where your home or room brings you joy without causing financial stress. This method also provides an opportunity to reflect on each potential purchase and determine if it truly sparks joy or if it's merely an impulse buy. Take the time to visualise the item in your space and consider how it makes you feel. Waiting for a month before making a purchase may even lead to discounted prices. However, keep in mind that if you come across a one-of-a-kind second-hand item, it might be bought by someone else, so consider that as well.

By being mindful of your budget and taking a thoughtful approach to adding new elements, you can create a space that truly reflects your preferences and brings you joy without putting a strain on your finances.

Overall, creating a space where you can truly express yourself is essential for your well-being. Whether it's your entire home, a specific room, or even just a corner of a room, it's important to focus on incorporating elements that you love and that bring you joy.

If you live with a partner, it's important to have open communication and come to an agreement on how both of you can create a space that reflects your individual tastes and desires. The same applies to living with roommates or family members. Even small changes, such as changing your duvet cover or adding personal touches, can have a significant impact on how you feel in your space. These adjustments allow your home to become a reflection of your unique personality and bring a sense of comfort and happiness.

Remember, it's not about the size or extravagance of the changes you make, but rather the personal meaning they hold for you. Embrace the opportunity to infuse your space with elements that bring you joy, and let your home become a place that truly represents who you are.

Enjoy your home life

While decorating your home according to your preferences can bring you some enjoyment, it's important to remember that true satisfaction comes from how you live your life within your home. You could have the perfect house but still not enjoy the experience of being there, ultimately leaving you unsatisfied. On the other hand, you may not be particularly fond of your living space, but if you create an enjoyable and fulfilling experience within your home, it can greatly improve your overall satisfaction.

The key to a fulfilling home life is finding a balance between your living environment and the way you live your life within it. Making small changes that align with your preferences and bring you joy can significantly enhance your experience at home. Remember, these changes don't have to be drastic or feel like a chore—they should be enjoyable and leave you feeling good.

By creating an environment that reflects your personality and values, and by engaging in activities that bring you fulfilment, you can cultivate a home life that leaves you feeling fulfilled, refreshed, and excited to embrace each new day. It's about finding that perfect blend where your living space and your daily experiences harmonise to create a sense of contentment and happiness.

The first step towards enhancing your home life is to engage in activities that you genuinely enjoy. While this may seem obvious, many people get caught up in their responsibilities and obligations, often forgetting or neglecting to make time for the things that bring them joy. It's essential to consciously prioritise and make an effort to incorporate enjoyable activities into your life.

In today's society, there can be a stigma around the notion of doing something simply for the fun of it. There's often a belief that our pursuits must always serve a purpose or generate income. As a result, many individuals feel guilty or hesitant about engaging in activities solely for their own pleasure. It's important to challenge this mindset and recognise that pursuing happiness and personal fulfilment is a valid and worthwhile endeavour.

Take a moment to reflect on the activities that genuinely bring you happiness, but that you may not engage in frequently because they're not seen as a priority. Consider why these sources of joy have taken a backseat in your life. Shouldn't your own happiness be a top priority? It's not about sacrificing other important aspects of your life, but rather creating space in your days to incorporate what you love and what brings you joy.

Imagine how fulfilling your life could be if it were filled with activities that make you feel good. By making your own happiness a priority and making time for the things you enjoy, you can experience a profound transformation in your overall well-being and satisfaction. Embracing activities that bring you joy will infuse your home life with positivity and create a sense of fulfilment that radiates into every aspect of your daily existence.

It's important to note that the activities you incorporate into your home life don't have to be extravagant. Even small, simple pleasures can have a significant impact on your overall well-being. For example, dedicating a few moments each day to reading a book or setting aside time once a month to host a special evening meal can bring immense joy and fulfilment.

Take some time to reflect on all the activities you genuinely enjoy but may not engage in frequently or would like to incorporate more into your life. Consider which ones you could realistically make room for on a weekly basis. If you have a busy schedule, examine if there are any fewer essential activities that you could replace with those that bring you pleasure. By consciously prioritising and making space for activities that bring you joy, you are investing in your own happiness and well-being.

Remember, these moments of pleasure and enjoyment are essential for your overall quality of life. They provide you with an opportunity to recharge, unwind, and find fulfilment within the comfort of your own home. Embracing these activities, whether big or small, will contribute to creating a home life that is filled with moments of joy, relaxation, and personal fulfilment.

In addition to incorporating enjoyable activities into your home life, it's crucial to prioritise relaxation and stress reduction. Allocating as little as 30 minutes each day to engage in a practice that helps you unwind can make a significant difference. This practice can take various forms, such as meditation, going for a walk, or engaging in a spiritual activity. It's worth noting that what works for one person may not work for another. The key is to identify what relaxes you and leaves you feeling better afterward.

For example, I know someone who finds playing video games to be an effective way to de-stress after a long day of work. The important thing is to find what works for you personally, regardless of whether it aligns with conventional methods or not. Once you have identified the activities that help you relax, you can take it a step further and create a small ritual or routine around them. This could involve lighting a candle, brewing a cup of tea, and enjoying some quiet time with spa music playing in the background. Remember, there are no strict rules here – the aim is to create a calming and rejuvenating experience tailored to your preferences.

Your home should be a sanctuary where you can unwind and find solace, and it often requires taking accountability and actively making time for relaxation. By exploring and merging the activities that have helped you relax in the past, you can design a personalised ritual or practice to alleviate stress. The goal is to cultivate an environment in which you feel calm, rejuvenated, and at peace.

Your home should be a sanctuary where you feel safe to be your authentic self. Throughout the day, you may need to adopt a customer service persona or conform to certain expectations at work, but when you return home, you should be able to shed those roles and embrace your true identity. Your home is where you can freely express yourself and be unapologetically you.

This sense of freedom and self-expression extends beyond just the physical aspects of decorating your house. It encompasses being true to yourself in every aspect of your life. Engage in activities you love, hold onto your beliefs and values, and engage in conversations about topics that resonate with your heart. Allow yourself to let loose and fully be yourself within the walls of your home.

Of course, it's important to note that being yourself shouldn't come at the expense of hurting others or disregarding their feelings. Respecting the boundaries and needs of others is crucial in creating a harmonious living environment. However, within those bounds, you should feel empowered to express your true self, embracing your uniqueness and individuality.

If you live alone or with people you trust, it may be easier to establish an environment where you can freely express yourself. However, if you find yourself in a situation where this is not the case, try to find moments within your home life where you can authentically be yourself. Whether it's through personal hobbies, private spaces, or connecting with supportive friends and family, seek out opportunities to let your true self shine.

Remember, your home should be a haven where you feel accepted and cherished for who you are. Embrace this freedom of expression, celebrate your individuality, and create a nurturing space that reflects your true essence.

I want you to think back to when you were younger. If you were like me, you may have imagined all the amazing things you would do once you moved out of your house for the first time. You probably envisioned how you would decorate your home and all the things you would do in it. It's likely you felt a surge of excitement when considering the endless possibilities.

Personally, I've always had a strong desire to host dinner parties and create delightful evenings filled with delicious food, beautifully decorated tables, and a warm atmosphere.

I want you to tap into that same feeling you may have had. And if you didn't have that experience, I want you to imagine having a fresh start, where you have the freedom to do anything you want and all the time in the world to do it in your own house. Who would you invite over? What activities would you engage in alone or with others? What delectable dishes would you prepare? And what outfit would you wear for these special occasions? Think about all the things that excite you and bring you joy. Now, take those ideas and see if you can incorporate them into your reality. It may not be an exact replica of your dreams, but what matters most is embracing the present moment, sharing laughter, and creating wonderful memories.

Your house should be a place where you feel good and truly enjoy your life. It is the very essence of what you call home. Home is what you make it. It

holds immense potential for you to transform it
into the best possible version.

Sharing a home

One of the factors that can greatly influence your experience of living in your home is the people you share it with, if indeed you have anyone to share it with. These individuals may include your partner, family members, or friends. Even if you have a good relationship with them, living together can sometimes lead to challenges. On the other hand, if you live alone, there may be moments of loneliness or the need for companionship. Each person's living situation is unique, and there are various scenarios that may not have been covered. In this chapter, I will provide guidance on how you can add a touch of romance to your life while at home, regardless of whether you live with others or live alone, with only your feline companion.

The essence of living your best life at home lies in feeling a sense of enjoyment and fulfilment. Living alone can offer more freedom in terms of personal choices and activities, as you don't have to be as mindful of housemates. However, if you believe that sharing your home with a partner would contribute to your best life, the current situation may not be ideal for you. When you share a home, there can be a sense of restriction, particularly in terms of how you decorate your space or how you spend your time. For instance, you may desire to spend a day baking cakes, but if you live with a parent who also needs to use the kitchen, compromises must be made. Ideally, we would all like the freedom to do as we please, but when sharing a home, it's important to find a balance and allocate time for different activities, creating a more harmonious outcome. Sharing the space equally becomes key in fostering a positive living environment.

The dynamics and relationships within your shared living space can significantly impact the quality of your home life. If you have a harmonious and positive relationship with your housemates, you are likely to enjoy your time at home. It can feel stress-free and create a pleasant atmosphere. However, this may not be the case for everyone. Sometimes, there may be conflicts or a lack of compatibility with someone in your household, leading to tension and increased stress levels. It can become challenging to unwind after a long day of work. In such situations, it is advisable to take action and address the issue, considering a change in living arrangements if you feel it is necessary. However, if the situation is manageable, such as occasional anger from a family member, it may not warrant moving out immediately. Instead, finding ways to handle such moments, like taking time alone to relax, can be helpful. It's important to acknowledge that these situations are part of being human, as we all experience emotions. Learning how to navigate other people's emotions while protecting your own can contribute to a sense of peace in your life. If you're dealing with negative connections within your household, referring back to the romanticising your relationships section of this book may provide guidance on navigating these challenges.

You and the people you share your house with need to have moments alone, as well as moments spent together to bond and enjoy your connections. You could do something as simple as having a movie or game night, eating meals together, and talking about your days. By arranging and making these plans happen, you will give everyone something to look forward to collectively. Taking turns to decide what activities to do each time gives everyone the opportunity to share what they enjoy with the rest of the household.

While it can be a lot of fun to have loved ones sharing a space with you and creating enjoyable moments together, it is equally important to have moments alone. These times allow you to relax, recharge, and focus on doing things just for yourself. In the long run, this helps maintain a smooth-running household. Furthermore, it's crucial to have your own space where you can relax and make it your own, especially if you have your own bedroom. However, if you share a bedroom with a sibling or someone else, it can be challenging. Growing up, I always shared a bedroom with my sister, and we had different interests. I preferred girly decor, while she was a huge fan of various things, leading to conflicting styles. This made it difficult for both of us to fully decorate the room in a way that made us happy and expressed ourselves. Nevertheless, we found a solution by splitting the room in half—I decorated one side according to my desires, and she did the same. Having our own spaces allowed us to express ourselves and pursue what brought us joy. This approach prevented any potential resentment in the long run, and we were fortunate that our parents allowed us this flexibility. We even painted the walls different colours to match our preferences. If you find yourself in a similar situation, this is something you could consider doing.

It can be slightly different if you are in a relationship and share the entire house with your partner. In such a case, you can make the decision to decorate separate rooms individually, giving each of you full creative freedom. This arrangement also provides you with dedicated spaces where you can spend time alone whenever you desire it. For instance, if one person loves cooking and enjoys spending their free time preparing delicious meals, they could take charge of decorating the kitchen to their liking. On the other hand, if the other person finds solace and enjoyment in the garden, they could be responsible for decorating it according to their preferences. Additionally, you can designate certain rooms as neutral spaces and incorporate both of your tastes in common areas like the living room and bedroom. This way, you can create a harmonious blend that reflects both of your styles and interests.

Regardless of who you live with, it is crucial that each person has a role in maintaining and functioning properly within the house, rather than relying solely on one individual. While this concept is explored further in the next chapter, it is important for every member of the household to contribute to the upkeep of the house and assist others when needed. This includes tasks such as cooking, cleaning, and other chores. By sharing these responsibilities, it helps prevent any feelings of resentment from building up. Additionally, if one person is struggling on a particular night due to a tough day, others can step in and help with their tasks, such as switching roles. Finding a system that works for everyone in the household to collectively care for the house will contribute to the smooth running of the household.

When it comes to sharing a house, especially for those living alone, it is essential to be mindful of who you invite into your home, even for a visit. Opening up your home to others means inviting them into your energetic space. If someone leaves you feeling great, happy, and reenergised, their positive energy can contribute to your home environment. Conversely, the same applies to negative energy. If you invite someone into your home who brings you down and drains your energy, that energy can linger even after they leave, creating an undesirable atmosphere. It's important to be mindful of this dynamic.

Take a moment to consider the kind of people and energy you would like to invite into your home. If it is necessary for someone to come over, you can find ways to cleanse the energy before and after their visit. Alternatively, you could try arranging to meet them in a neutral space such as a café, where the energy of your home won't be affected. Being conscious of the energy you allow into your living space can contribute to a more positive and harmonious environment.

The people you share your home with can certainly influence your experience of home life, but it's important to acknowledge that there will always be negative factors involved, such as bills and chores. In the next chapter, we will explore ways to approach these aspects in a manner that allows you to find enjoyment and avoid unnecessary stress.

Romanticise the bad bits.

Living in your house comes with its fair share of perks, as we've discussed earlier. However, there are also aspects that may not be so enjoyable. In this chapter, we will explore strategies to make those less pleasant parts more bearable, and perhaps even enjoyable.

You may find that some of the techniques and ideas mentioned here are repetitive. However, repetition is in fact beneficial as it helps reinforce the information and strategies in your mind. So, I encourage you to stick with this chapter and embrace the potential benefits it can bring you.

Doing chores is a necessary part of maintaining a household, and while some tasks may be enjoyable, there are likely a few that you'd prefer to avoid. I'll keep this section concise, as we've discussed various ways to make chores more enjoyable earlier in the book. As a recap, you can find ways to make chores pleasurable, such as listening to music or a podcast while you work.

Try combining activities you already enjoy with these tasks to find fulfilment in them.

If you find your chores list becoming overwhelming, there are two approaches you can consider. First, you could dedicate a specific day to tackle all your chores, and at the end of the day, reward yourself with something that makes it all feel worthwhile. Throughout the day, you can find small pleasures to incorporate into your tasks, like lighting a scented candle or wearing comfortable clothes that make you feel good. Your final chore could be going food shopping, where you can buy yourself a treat like flowers to brighten up your space, a sweet indulgence, or a nice drink to enjoy. This can serve as a reward for your hard work and give you a sense of accomplishment, knowing that you won't have to worry about certain tasks for a little while.

If the idea of dedicating a whole day to chores feels overwhelming or if you have a busy schedule, another approach you can take is to create a daily list of three tasks that need to be done. By incorporating these tasks into your other activities, you give yourself breaks in between and avoid feeling overwhelmed. During these breaks, you can engage in activities you enjoy, knowing that once you complete a task, you can reward yourself with something that brings you happiness.

While you're doing the chores, you can make them more enjoyable by multitasking. For example, you can listen to an audiobook or call a friend while cleaning or organising. This way, you can make the most of your time and engage in activities that bring you fulfilment.

By following this approach, you'll not only accomplish your daily chores but also have time for other activities. At the end of the day, you'll feel a sense of accomplishment knowing that you've balanced your responsibilities with enjoyable moments throughout the day.

When sharing a house with others, it's important to ensure that the load of chores is shared among everyone. You can make chores enjoyable by doing them together as a group. Play some music and sing along while you clean, creating a fun and lively atmosphere. If you find yourself being the only one doing the chores, it's essential to communicate with your housemates and express your desire for help. By discussing it openly, you can make it easier for everyone to contribute and turn chores into a shared responsibility.

This reminds me of a memory from my childhood when my siblings and I made a big mess with our toys. We didn't want to clean it up, but my mum turned it into a game. She asked us to pick up items of a specific colour and put them back in the toy box. Each colour became a different challenge. Without realising it, we were tidying up while enjoying the game. You can try incorporating games into your chores as well. It may require some creativity, but it can transform the tasks into something more enjoyable and engaging.

Another not-so-enjoyable part of living in a house is paying rent and bills. To be honest, I haven't discovered a way to make this task fun and enjoyable because, let's face it, everyone would rather use their money for something else. It can be quite stressful, especially when your financial situation isn't ideal. Instead of trying to romanticise or make it fun, I suggest shifting your perspective and cultivating a sense of gratitude for what you are paying for. When you pay your rent, express gratitude for having a comfortable home and a place to relax and unwind. Similarly, when paying for food, appreciate the fact that you have nourishment, and perhaps it's even something delicious! By embracing gratitude for the things, you are paying for, you may find a greater sense of peace towards these bills. Now, when it comes to tasks like writing emails or filing taxes, you can transform the experience into a luxury one. Treat yourself to a lovely drink, create a cosy ambiance with candlelight, and play beautiful classical music in the background. By associating these chores with positive elements, you can make them more enjoyable and elevate the overall experience.

Whatever part of your home life isn't ideal and doesn't make you feel like you are thriving, there are ways to try and counteract those feelings with joy. Finding ways to bring joy and happiness into your home life, will make the difficult parts easier for you.

Overall

The key is to prioritise making your home life enjoyable and peaceful. Your home should be a place where you feel good, relaxed, and safe. If you feel that there are areas that could be improved, start by asking yourself a simple question: "What could I do to make myself feel good right now?" It's common to initially feel stuck or lack inspiration, but by using the chapters in this book as a guide, you can gain valuable ideas and insights on the actions you can take to enhance your living environment. Remember, small changes and adjustments can make a significant difference in creating a space that brings you joy and contentment.

As I have mentioned several times before, you have the power to shape your life, including your home life, into whatever you desire. The beauty of life lies in the fact that each passing minute offers a fresh opportunity to start anew and make positive changes. Once you've completed this chapter, I encourage you to engage in activities within your home that bring you immense joy. Consider rearranging elements in your room to create a space that truly uplifts your spirit. If you're struggling for ideas, take a closer look at life itself and discover inspiration and beauty in the simplicity of home life. Social media and the internet are also excellent sources for finding creative concepts. I urge you to embrace the boundless possibilities for transforming your home life. Do you have any ideas for redecorating your home? Perhaps you can explore engaging activities with the other occupants of your home. Now is an exciting moment for you to discover ways to flourish in your home life. Even more so, it is the perfect time to take action and thrive in every aspect of your life.

Final Thoughts

Romanticising your life

You might find it surprising to learn that there is no magical or secret formula for living your best life and finding joy in it. Much of what I've shared is simple and may even be concepts you've come across before from others. Many people are constantly searching for the next big thing to improve their lives, believing that the key lies in something obscure and complex. In this pursuit, we often overlook the simple things that truly matter. These simple solutions may seem too straightforward to be the answer. Society has conditioned us to believe that attaining the best things in life requires following a convoluted path accessible only to a select few. However, practices such as gratitude and mindfulness are taught and embraced everywhere because they have the power to profoundly impact our lives when consistently applied.

It's easy to become fixated on the major aspects of life, such as relationships, career, money, and home life, when seeking improvements. However, it's important to recognise that numerous small things also contribute significantly to how we experience life. The best moments of your day can stem from simple pleasures like enjoying a delicious drink, having a pleasant commute, or wearing a stylish outfit. You wouldn't believe the excitement and joy I feel when I discover and light a vanilla-scented candle. Engaging in small actions that bring you pleasure can have a profound impact. You can elevate the experience of eating by presenting your food in an appealing way or sip your drink from a fancy teacup. (I've recently started doing this, and it brings me immense joy.) These seemingly insignificant details can bring about happiness in unexpected ways.

Challenge yourself to actively seek out and embrace small joys in your life. Cultivate mindfulness and develop an appreciation for the inherent beauty in everything around you. Strive to surround yourself only with things that bring you joy, whether it be your possessions, activities, or the company you keep. The essence of romanticising your life lies in prioritising your own happiness. Make a conscious effort to put yourself first and strive to make each moment the best it can be. By doing so, you'll discover the power of infusing joy and enchantment into your everyday experiences.

Throughout my journey of dealing with anxiety and the process of writing this book, I have gained valuable insights and learned numerous lessons. By putting into practice the principles I've shared, I've opened myself up to wonderful opportunities and embraced vibrant new changes. It has empowered me to live life authentically, following my heart and pursuing what brings me joy. We are all united in the experience of being human, navigating the ups and downs of life's journey. Let us support and uplift one another as we strive to create fulfilling and meaningful lives.

Now is the time for reflection and personal evaluation. As you reach the end of this book, it's crucial to take accountability for your own life and actively implement the changes and value you've discovered. Your journey towards living your best life starts with you. This book will always serve as a guide, providing inspiration and ideas for your path forward. Take a moment to envision what you want your life to look like in five years. Visualise the person you aspire to become. The key to reaching that future is to embody that version of yourself now. Make decisions with the perspective of the person living their dream life. Consider whether the future you would be satisfied if you chose to remain stagnant and took no action. Embrace the essence of that desired person and lifestyle, and you will witness your reality aligning with your desires. It's time to take ownership and make the necessary changes to shape your reality.

I believe that we should let our hearts and happiness guide us. Everyone deserves to live a life where they are happy and can enjoy the present moment. And, in my opinion, that is the core essence of romanticising your life: leading it with love, happiness, and being mindful of the beauty that surrounds us. Start romanticising your life now, and witness how truly beautiful life can be.

Acknowledgements

There are many people I could thank for being a part of the process for writing this book. This is of course, my first ever book and this took a long time to write, edit, and self-publish. Some of these people are no longer in my life anymore.

Firstly, I would like to thank my family. My Mum, Dad, Lauren, and Harry. You have always been there for me and have been supportive of my journey. Helping me proofread this book. My friends, Molly and Nann. You two have been so loyal and encourage me to keep going. You both have been a huge part of my wellness and spiritual journey.

I would also like to thank Matthew, for being there every step of the way, being the perfect partner that I could ever ask for. I would also like to thank his family, Debbie, Mick, and Ruth for sharing the excitement with this book.

I also want to express my gratitude towards Kindle Direct Publishing for creating this platform to allow me to publish this book.

I would like to thank my old University Lecturer Mark, you have inspired me immensely when it came to my writing of this book and encouraging with my path in life.

Finally, I want to thank each and every individual who were a part of my journey on social media who supported me whilst I was documenting my process of self-publishing. The kind messages of support have inspired me immensely to keep going. Those who let me appear on their podcast to talk about my book, I'm genuinely grateful.

About the author

Honor Lewis is a 23-year-old upcoming author and transformational guide who discovered the power of the Law of Attraction at a young age, forever changing the trajectory of her life. Through her profound personal journey and unwavering commitment to self-discovery, she has become a beacon of inspiration, guiding others to embrace their true potential and live their desired reality.

At the tender age of 17, Honor encountered a pivotal moment in her life when she was gifted a book on the Law of Attraction by a mysterious lady. Struggling with depression and anxiety at the time, this fortuitous encounter ignited a spark within her and set her on a path of profound transformation. It opened her eyes to the immense power we all possess to shape our own destinies and create lives filled with love, joy, and purpose.

Building upon her newfound passion for personal growth and spiritual exploration, Honor immersed herself in the study and practice of self-help, tarot reading, and manifestation. Recognising the profound impact these tools had on her own life, she dedicated herself to becoming a trusted guide for others seeking to unlock their own potential and manifest their dreams. With a unique blend of intuition, empathy, and deep spiritual understanding, Honor has helped countless individuals navigate their personal journeys and step into their authentic selves.

With a burning desire to make a positive impact on the lives of others, Honor Lewis has dedicated her life's work to helping individuals live their best lives and pursue their dreams. As a manifestation coach, she has honed her expertise in guiding others through the process of intentional creation and empowering them to overcome limiting beliefs. Through her compassionate and insightful approach, Honor has become a trusted mentor and source of inspiration for those seeking to embrace their passions, unleash their creativity, and live a life of fulfilment. She does this through her social media called Honor's Diary. Showcasing her journey of life.

Honor Lewis's unwavering commitment to empowering individuals to live their best lives and follow their dreams shines through in her writing. Her genuine passion for helping others, coupled with her relatability and compassionate approach, make her the ideal guide to inspire readers to embrace the art of romanticising life and manifest their desired realities.

Bibliography

1. Encyclopedia Britannica. 2022.
    Romanticism | Definition, Characteristics,
    connections, History, Art, Poetry,
    Literature, & Music. [online] Available at:
    <https://www.britannica.com/art/Romanti
    cism> [Accessed 27 February 2022].

2. Campbell, L., 2022. What Does It Mean to
    Be an Empath?. [online] Verywell Mind.
    Available at:
    <https://www.verywellmind.com/what-is-
    an-empath-and-how-do-you-know-if-you-
    are-one-5119883> [Accessed 29 September
    2022].

3. Susman, D., 2022. Clutter and Mental
    Health: What's the Connection?. [online]
    Verywell Mind. Available at:
    <https://www.verywellmind.com/declutter

ing-our-house-to-cleanse-our-minds-5101511> [Accessed 5 October 2022].

4. Feelings: The perception of the self – James Laired

5. Scott PHD, E., 2020. What is the law of attraction. [online] Verywell Mind. Available at: <https://www.verywellmind.com/understanding-and-using-the-law-of-attraction-3144808> [Accessed 11 April 2022].

Printed in Dunstable, United Kingdom